The Grumpy Programmer's Guide
To Testing PHP Applications

by Chris Hartjes

The Grumpy Programmer's Guide To Testing PHP Applications

php[architect] edition published: May 2020

Print ISBN:	978-1-940111-79-7
PDF ISBN:	978-1-940111-80-3
ePub ISBN:	978-1-940111-81-0
Mobi ISBN	978-1-940111-82-7

Produced & Printed in the United States

Written by
Chris Hartjes

Editor
Kara Ferguson

Layout
Oscar Merida

Published by
musketeers.me, LLC.
4627 University Dr
Fairfax, VA 22030 USA

240-348-5PHP (240-348-5747)
info@phparch.com
www.phparch.com

Table of Contents

1. Introduction   1

2. Changing How We Think About Tests   5
    It's A Funnel, Not A Pyramid.   6
    Customer Tests and Developer Tests   7

3. What Are Tests?   9
    Prerequisites   11
    Manual Tests   11
    Semi-Automated Tests Using Real Dependencies   11
    Semi-Automated Tests Using Test Doubles   12
    Automated Tests   12
    Final Thoughts   13

4. How PHPUnit Works   15
    High-Level Overview   15
    How Do We Install PHPUnit?   16
    The PHPUnit Test Runner   17
    PHPUnit Test Cases   21

5. Test Double   25
    What Is a Test Double?   25
    Dummies   26
    Test Stub   27
    Mock Objects and Test Spies   28
    Fakes   36
    Final Thoughts   40

6. Test-Driven Development by Example   41

Tooling   42

Getting Started   42

First Test   44

Next Test   46

Building Further Test Cases   48

Refactoring The Tests   49

Handling Non-Valid Input   55

Final Thoughts   57

7. Test-After Development by Example   59

What's the Difference?   59

What Is the Expected Behavior?   60

How Am I Going to Test This?   61

8. Refactoring Helpers   69

9. Testing APIs   73

Response Validation   74

API Schema Validation   77

10. Data Providers   83

Why You Should Use Data Providers   83

Look at All Those Tests   84

Creating Data Providers   85

More Complex Examples   86

Data Provider Tricks   87

Final Thoughts   88

11. Wrappers   89

    Wrappers From Up High   90

12. Metatesting   95

    Mature Testing Tools Are Available   96

    Open Source Drives Acceptance   97

    Proof Exists to Back the Promises   97

    Testing Moves Bug Fixing to a Cheaper Part of the Cycle   97

    Well-Documented Build Systems Encourage Continuous Deployment 98

    There Are Awesome Complementary Tools   100

13. Building a Testing Culture   107

    Primary Goal   108

    Tests as First Class Components   108

    Tests for Bugs   108

    Tests for New Features   109

    Tests for Refactoring   110

    Commitment to Peer Review   110

    Consistency in Development Environments   111

    Automation Is Your Friend   111

    Same Languages and Tools   112

    Same Practices   112

    Trust   113

14. Bootstrapping   115

    Test Environment Bootstrapping   117

    Auto-Wiring Bootstrapping   120

15. No Tests? No Problem!   123

How Did We End Up Without Any Tests?   124

Bug Fixes Need Proof   124

New Features Require Proof   125

Test Suites Are Not Bulletproof   125

16. Nobody Is Running the Tests!   127

Time Pressure   128

Tests Are Too Slow   128

Monolithic Bootstrapping   129

Shared Testing Environments   129

17. "You're Not Getting Paid to Test!"   131

Testing Is Part of the Job   132

Lost Opportunity Costs   132

18. It's About People   135

Like Kids on a Playground   136

Lack of Good Docs   136

Convincing People About Time   137

Cowboys Above Me   138

Index   139

Chapter

1

Introduction

I've been trying to help people test their PHP code for a very long time, probably before some of you reading this book even got started in programming. PHPUnit didn't exist, the most commonly-used version of PHP was 5.0, and social media wasn't a thing. Google didn't even exist. My first search engine was AltaVista. Yes, I learned to test uphill, both ways, in the snow.

My own experiences with testing came out of a terrible launch of a terrible product in the spring of 2003. I spent a full calendar year helping build a PHP and MySQL application that was an adult dating site. It was a very typical PHP application of its time–business logic mixed in with presentation logic in the "spaghetti-style" many people associate with PHP. To this, we added a layer of web application servers, the use of MySQL replication, and the use of a queue to handle writing data to MySQL. In many ways, it was quite ahead of its time.

Of course, it was a disaster. The launch went poorly, there were lots of errors, and the team lead for the developers was the scapegoat for the poor launch. We did have a QA department, but their work was ineffective and thankless. No coordination between the developers and these folks testing the application in the browser combined with poor communication meant things were always going to be adversarial.

In the aftermath of this launch, I was called into the project manager's office for a meeting. After a discussion that ended with him saying, "Well, we're not going to need *this*," and threw an envelope containing a termination letter and a severance check into the trash, he handed me a copy of a book and said, "I'd like you to spend the weekend looking at this book and let me know what you think on Monday morning." That book was a copy of "Extreme Programming Installed" by Ron Jeffries, Ann Anderson, and Chet Hendrickson. At the time, I was commuting from the outer fringes of the Greater Toronto Area, taking the commuter train for 90 minutes in and 2 hours home (due to connections). I had lots of time to take a look at this book.

You rarely run across a concept that actually changes your life as an adult. In this case, when I read the sections of the book about unit testing, I was stunned and excited. There was a way we could use the computer itself to find mistakes and bugs in our code instead of relying on QA folks or our customers? This was revolutionary to me despite me being five years into getting paid to write computer programs.

When I got back to work and met again with that project manager, plans were made to start attacking the problems we were facing in the application and get some sort of tests in place. Not too long afterward, I wrote my first unit test using the SimpleTest framework (basically PHPUnit, but the tests ran in the browser), and the rest is a test-centric career.

Testing, as a concept, is hard to explain to beginning programmers: "We are going to write code that is going to make sure your other code works as expected." The assumption underlying all this is that you already understand how to write computer programs in your chosen language! This makes it very difficult to teach to beginner or inexperienced programmers. When you combine this with how PHP does not force any particular structure on you, you have an environment where only the folks who are really motivated learn about testing.

There is something like "survivorship bias" at play here, too. The people who latch onto testing as a practice to incorporate into their development workflow are those who have had success with it. We seldom hear from folks who tried to learn testing (either on their own or from others) and have not had success with it. In general, the testing community is small but quite vocal about their opinions. I can understand people hesitating to share their lack of success.

This book is my way of providing some help for developers who are looking to become more test-centric. By learning the basic skills (both technical and non-technical), you will be able to write tests using almost any testing framework and almost any PHP application.

We're going to start by taking a look at what a test actually is because I feel many people (including experienced testers) are misguided as to the target of a test. After that, we'll take a look at how PHPUnit works so you can understand better ways of using it. Armed with that knowledge, we will use Test-Driven Development (TDD) to build some code to illustrate how tests can be used to drive the design of your application's code.

Most of us are not lucky enough to be in a position to use TDD on a new project. I will show you how to write tests for an existing application, especially one that was not written with any tests in mind. The tools are the same; we just use them differently.

After having written some tests, we will then move onto dealing with the people side of testing by providing strategies to help get the people you work with to become more test-centric. Understanding that testing was more about people than the tools themselves was a major revelation for me.

To get the most out of this book, you should be a developer who has an intermediate understanding of PHP. It's hard to write tests when you don't have a firm grasp of the language itself, and the types of tests you'll be writing are more PHP code you will need to understand and support.

Good luck and I hope you find the material in here useful. I would love to hear your feedback as you work your way through this book. The best way to reach me is via Twitter, where I do performance art as @grmpyprogrammer. If Twitter (or social media in general) is not your thing, you can email me at chartjes@grumpy-learning.com. I read every email that is not labeled as spam and try and answer them as soon as I can.

Chapter

2

Changing How We Think About Tests

Software testing as an "acceptable" practice has been around for almost 20 years. Setting aside the fact that most of the testing problems we face today were solved by people in the 1970s (my copy of Boris Beizer's "Software Testing Techniques" was first published in 1982), many developers have a pretty good idea about how automated testing, in general, works. They might want to argue about "the testing pyramid" or "unit versus integration versus functional" testing. Before we dive headlong into testing concepts, I want to change what you think about tests at a very high level.

It's A Funnel, Not A Pyramid.

One mental construct you can use for "how many and what kind of tests do we need" is the concept of a testing pyramid. It sort of looks like this:

In a blog post[1], Martin Fowler credits Mike Cohn's book "Succeeding with Agile" as the source. That blog post is a great look at one overall strategy for approaching writing tests of different kinds and for different purposes.

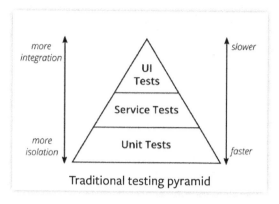

Traditional testing pyramid

The labels on the pyramid are often "unit", "integration", and "functional." On top of this, the pyramid seems to imply there is some kind of desirable ratio between the layers. Taken to an extreme, people (including me) sometimes fall into the trap of making poorly-thought-out generalizations like "90 unit, 9 integration, 1 functional" as a rule of thumb for organizing your tests suites. After all, you only want to write the "correct" number of tests, right?

Then, one day, Noah Sussman, @noahsussman shared this image that has resonated with me ever since.

What really hit home was this idea of "only bugs not reducible by get here." All of those different filters serve different purposes! There is no magic ratio, only a vague sense of "I think I've written enough of these," for a developer to go with. This is why good test suites are the byproduct of many years of making mistakes!

Noah Sussman's testing filters

Thinking of the tests as filters will also go a long way toward reducing the number of tests in each layer that do the same thing. Each test should have a purpose–and I am not talking about, "so we have 100% coverage of every line of code!" That is a nice side-effect, but that sort of thinking leads to test suites that we think are doing the job but no longer reflect how the application actually works.

---

[1]   blog post: https://martinfowler.com/articles/practical-test-pyramid.html

As you get deeper into my book, think of these tests as filters of different types–they are looking to stop different types of bugs from happening but have the same goal of an application reaching production with the fewest bugs possible.

Customer Tests and Developer Tests

Once again, let's go back to the labeling and purposes of some tests. One way they have been labeled is "unit", "integration", and "functional." Those are great descriptions of what the tests are but not what they are for. There is a difference!

Let's dig into the definitions I like to use when referring to tests for PHP code:

- A "unit" test is one which verifies the behavior of a single method of an object that is part of an application, often using doubles in the place of dependencies for the code under test.

- An "integration" test is one which verifies the behavior of a small number of objects that are part of an application, when used together and without the use of doubles of dependencies for the code under test.

- A "functional" test is one which verifies a small subset of behavior of the application as a whole by using the application itself along with some kind of automation (usually web browser-based).

Instead, I want you to consider a different way of grouping these tests: customer tests and developer tests. This method puts the two different groups that have a real stake in the success of the application at the forefront of the discussion.

Customer tests are any test that proves your application is behaving in a way that the customer expects it to. This would cover what we traditionally think of "functional" or "UI" tests. Here's a classic example: A test that verifies you can create an account and then perform some common action. That is 100% a test for a customer. Feel free to substitute "user" for "customer" if it feels better to you. The point is we are testing the application itself via customer tests.

Developer tests are any tests that prove a specific set of code is behaving the way the developer expects it to. This would cover what we traditionally think of as "unit" or "integration" tests. What does a customer care about a unit test? Why should they care about it at all? What they care about is, "Does this application work the way I expect it too and solve the problems I am trying to solve with it?" Any attempt to justify that users of a system care how well-tested it is, is naive at best, egotistical at worst. The goal of the developer test is to guide anyone working with the application at a coding level to create testing scenarios that ensure the code, at the lowest level we care about, is functioning.

Chapter

3

What Are Tests?

There are several ways we can answer this question. When I was first learning to write tests, I didn't really think much about it. I wrote some code, used the test runner, and looked to see if I got the expected results. If we back up a bit, I think we can get a much more useful answer.

From a very high level, a test is code you have written which confirms the code you are trying to test is behaving as expected. It's a very simple concept. Everything else used to describe what a test is, builds on this foundation.

If you look at it another way, there's a question you should ask yourself every time you write code: How can I prove this code behaves the way I am expecting it to? By focusing on making sure behavior is tested instead of lines of code, we end up with test suites that are more focused on the task of being proofs instead of something we do to target an often-arbitrary "How much of our code is covered by tests?" number.

Before I start talking about the different levels of tests you might end up creating, I wanted to share a story about the effectiveness of tests and TDD (Test-Driven Development), in particular.

In June 2008, a paper about the effectiveness of TDD was published. The paper discussed case studies of how IBM and Microsoft experimented with TDD by giving teams the same programming tasks but asking some of them to use TDD as opposed to no formalized testing practices at all.

The teams that used TDD took 15% to 35% longer in terms of development time. This is not surprising because tests are code you write to prove other code is behaving correctly. It is likely to take more time, so this result lines up with my own personal experiences.

The teams that used TDD saw a 40% to 90% decrease in the number of defects in their code as compared to teams not using it. To me, this is the big win you get from having tests for your application. Having something that can actively prevent defects from being released to production is a big win.

We are at a point in software development where there is a big rush to "get something out there" or "you gotta release a Minimum Viable Product." Notice how "make sure stuff is working correctly for your use cases" is missing from any of this advice. Offloading testing onto the users of our applications is a terrible trend that seems to be picking up steam. By learning the skills you need to write tests, you can help reverse this trend.

I want to share what I feel is a progression of the types of tests you will end up creating for your application. The end goal is always the same: A repeatable process that ensures your code continues to behave the way you expect it to. This does not necessarily mean that no bugs occur, although the use of tests greatly reduces the bugs your users might run into. In this list, I mention some testing concepts you might not be familiar with but are addressed later in the book. Don't worry or feel intimidated!

Prerequisites

Before you can start writing tests, there are some other things you need to have in place to make these tests worth doing. First, you need to have some way to revert changes to the code for the application. Hopefully, you are using some sort of version control system. Git is currently the industry standard, and you can find lots of information online on how to use Git and tools that are designed to work with it.

The next thing you will need is some way to apply and roll back any changes you make to your data storage tools. It doesn't matter if it's a relational database or a key-value store or a document database–if you cannot roll back the changes you make to data or the schema you are using to guide organizing the data, you will constantly run into situations where you cannot go back.

There are PHP tools available to help you with database migrations (what the changes you make to data sources are commonly referred to as), and many popular object-relation mappers (ORMs) come with tools to manage them.

I cannot emphasize enough that you need to have procedures to roll back changes in place before you even attempt to get tests in place.

Manual Tests

If you have no tests in place, the first tests you should be writing are checklists for someone to manually follow. These tests should be having someone actually use your application and perform one or more tasks to make sure features of your application are behaving as expected. I usually advise people to begin with these checklists for the functionality of your application that absolutely has to work as expected 100% of the time.

If any of these tests fail, you should be rolling back the changes you made and returning the application to its previous state. Then, run through your checklist again and make sure the tests still pass. Once you've verified the bug exists, it's time to get someone to fix it, reapply the changes, and run through the checklist again. If the bug is still there, roll back again and keep repeating the process until the application passes your checklist test.

Semi-Automated Tests Using Real Dependencies

The next step after manual testing is to start using a PHP testing framework (I use PHPUnit) to write tests that verify the behavior of your code and use real dependencies instead of creating substitutes for them, which are more commonly known as test doubles. We're going to cover test doubles later in the book, but let's keep going.

This is the biggest obstacle you will face as you learn to use tools to create tests-as-code. The terminology is unclear, the tools seem intimidating, and you don't know where to start. In a different chapter, I cover creating tests from scratch, but at this point, think of these tests as black boxes generating pass or fail responses.

These tests end up looking very similar to the actual code in your application. In fact, your existing code is the first template you can use for tests written using a testing framework! Starting with cutting-and-pasting code from your application into a test and then adding an assertion (a statement that determines if a condition is true) is the first building block for a test suite.

So why do I call this step semi-automated? PHPUnit (and other PHP testing frameworks) can run from the command line. If you have some tests in place, someone can get your code with applied changes from version control, and run the tests from the command line manually. This last step still requires a human.

Semi-Automated Tests Using Test Doubles

When teaching people how to write tests, I encourage them to use the "real" version of dependencies. However, there are times when you need to substitute a real dependency (like a database or the results of an API call) with one you can control every aspect of. I will cover test doubles, so no need to worry about the nuts-and-bolts of them.

At this stage, we are re-examining the tests we have already written and deciding which of the dependencies for our tests we need to turn into test doubles. Modify your tests as required, and then run them via your CLI (command line interface).

Automated Tests

The final stage of the tests are ones that can be run via tools which encourage automation. These are usually described as build servers or continuous integration servers. No matter what you call them, their job is to perform automated tasks for you. Here is a typical set of actions that incorporate a build server:

- You commit your changes into the version control system
- The version control system sends a signal to your build server
- The build server receives the signal and starts its automated tasks
- It grabs a copy of your code from version control including your changes
- It does any work it needs to in order to create an environment for your code to run in
- It runs your tests

- It reports back if it passed or failed

One of the advantages of getting to this final stage is you are taking advantage of something that computers are very good at, doing what you tell them to do over and over again, usually without complaining. So if I can get another computer to react to what I am doing and run my tests for me, I can concentrate on solving problems instead of remembering a sequence of commands that I have a high probability of accidentally messing up.

Final Thoughts

The purpose of tests is to give you the confidence that any defects that make it into your code are detected before the application makes it up into production. That confidence also allows you to refactor or rewrite your code with the knowledge that if you accidentally break something that was previously working, you'll know before your users do.

Chapter

4

How PHPUnit Works

High-Level Overview

While PHPUnit wasn't the first testing framework I used (that honor belongs to SimpleTest), it is the framework I use most often. There are many other tools out there for testing your code, but I keep coming back to PHPUnit for the simplicity of its approach and the wide variety of add-ons others have created to make it even more useful.

PHPUnit is a collection of tools consisting of a testing framework and some command-line utilities which allow you to run tests written in PHP. Originally developed by Sebastian Bergmann, it has grown to have many contributors and is still under active development.

PHPUnit uses what is known as the xUnit architecture for its tools. xUnit has a number of conventions which lead you to build tests a specific way through the use of assertions. Assertions (a built-in feature of PHP) are statements which assert that a particular condition is true or false, depending on the goal of the testing scenario you have created.

The Wikipedia article on xUnit contains a nice summary, but here are the parts we need to worry about:

- test runner
- test cases
- test suites

Before we can look at those, we need to install PHPUnit.

How Do We Install PHPUnit?

The PHPUnit website is the best source of truthiness for anything to do with PHPUnit. Before you install it, make sure to check the website for any requirements. As I am writing this book, the current version of PHPUnit is 8.4. Assuming you have met the minimum requirements for it, there are two ways to install PHPUnit.

Install via PHP Archive (PHAR)

The PHAR version of PHPUnit is a binary you download and install somewhere in your path. To use it, you must also have the phar extension installed and enabled for PHP. PHPUnit recommends downloading the PHAR version and making it available locally for your project as opposed to being installed globally.

PHPUnit also recommends not having PHPUnit installed in a production environment. Tools with CLI (command-line interface) components can be exploited through vulnerabilities in other libraries, and there is a non-zero chance that a determined attacker can learn something from seeing the output of the test run.

I am not a security expert, but why give people opportunities to mess around with your application?

Install via Composer

Composer is the PHP community's tool for installing PHP-related packages and their associated dependencies. It is highly recommended to install PHPUnit using Composer as a development-time dependency only. Again, we want to avoid installing anything to do with PHPUnit in production.

Assuming you have installed Composer, you can add PHPUnit to your project with the following CLI command via your shell. This will install any version of PHPUnit that is 8.4 and above that fits with your current dependencies.

```
composer require ---dev phpunit/phpunit ^8.4`
```

With PHPUnit installed, we can take a look at how to execute the test cases you're going to write.

The PHPUnit Test Runner

The test runner is a CLI tool used to execute your test cases and report back the results of those tests. To use PHPUnit, you need to become familiar with using CLIs for your operating system of choice.

The test runner has a number of parameters you should be aware of. Like many powerful tools, there are a wide range of options; you will find yourself using only a small subset of those available.

At its most basic, you use the command `phpunit` from your shell (this assumes you either specify the complete path to where `phpunit` is, or it's in your shell's execution path). It then starts recursive searching from either your current directory (the default) or from the path you specify for files with a `.php` extension.

If those files contain an object that extends from one of PHPUnit's base test case classes, PHPUnit then tries to execute any class methods it recognizes as tests. By default, it assumes any method starting with test is supposed to be a test case, and tries to execute the code in it. You can also use DocBlocks with annotations in them to indicate a class method is supposed to be a test. There are some examples of this later in the book.

The test runner will execute those tests, continuing to try and execute anything it thinks it is a test until it cannot find any more of them.

Here's a little demonstration of how the runner works. First, you need to create the simplest test case possible. Don't worry; you'll get into the basics of test cases later in the book. We just need a placeholder for now. Once you have PHPUnit installed, create the following file and call it BasicTestCase.php

```
 1. <?php
 2.
 3. declare(strict_types=1);
 4.
 5. class BasicTestCase extends PHPUnit\Framework\TestCase
 6. {
 7.     public function testCase()
 8.     {
 9.         $this->assertTrue(false);
10.     }
11. }
```

Next, use the CLI test runner. You should get something very similar to the following output:

```
> phpunit BasicTestCase.php
PHPUnit 8.3.4 by Sebastian Bergmann and contributors.

F                                                          1 / 1
(100%)

Time: 91 ms, Memory: 12.00 MB

There was 1 failure:

1) BasicTestCase::testCase
Failed asserting that false is true.

/Users/chartjes/grumpy-guide/test/basic_test_case.php:9

FAILURES!
Tests: 1, Assertions: 1, Failures: 1.
```

As you can see, the test runner tells us:

- The status of the test (in this case F for fail)
- How long it took
- How much memory was consumed
- Outlines the exact failure and helpfully includes the line
- How many tests and how many assertions it contains

Now create a passing test case so you can see the difference:

```php
1. <?php
2.
3. declare(strict_types=1);
4.
5. class BasicTestCase extends PHPUnit\Framework\TestCase
6. {
7.     public function testCase()
8.     {
9.         $this->assertTrue(true);
10.     }
11. }
```

Then, use the test runner and run this test.

```
PHPUnit 8.3.4 by Sebastian Bergmann and contributors.

.                                                          1 / 1
(100%)

Time: 97 ms, Memory: 12.00 MB

OK (1 test, 1 assertion)
```

The test runner now shows you less information but informs you that the one assertion in your one test passed. What happens if you add another assertion?

```php
1. <?php
2.
3. declare(strict_types=1);
4.
5. class BasicTestCase extends PHPUnit\Framework\TestCase
6. {
7.     public function testCase()
8.     {
9.         $this->assertTrue(true);
10.             $this->assertFalse(false);
11.     }
12. }
```

Once again, use the test runner to run the test.

```
phpunit BasicTestCase.php
PHPUnit 8.3.4 by Sebastian Bergmann and contributors.

.                                                              1 / 1
(100%)

Time: 135 ms, Memory: 12.00 MB

OK (1 test, 2 assertions)
```

Similar messages, and now it indicates you have one test with two assertions, both of which behave as expected.

One more small tweak — edit your basic test case file to have two test methods in it.

```
1.  <?php
2.
3.  declare(strict_types=1);
4.
5.  class BasicTestCase extends PHPUnit\Framework\TestCase
6.  {
7.      public function testCase()
8.      {
9.          $this->assertTrue(true);
10.     }
11.
12.     public function testAnotherTestCase()
13.     {
14.         $this->assertFalse(false);
15.     }
16. }
```

Here's the output from the test runner. Can you spot the difference?

```
> phpunit BasicTestCase.php
PHPUnit 8.3.4 by Sebastian Bergmann and contributors.

..                                                             2 / 2
(100%)

Time: 101 ms, Memory: 12.00 MB

OK (2 tests, 2 assertions)
```

PHPUnit's default test runner output provides you with enough details that you can figure out what tests are failing and can also be used as a sanity check to make sure the number of tests and assertions you have written is correct. PHPUnit provides you with many options for changing the display output. Again, I'll get into those later on in the book.

PHPUnit Test Cases

We've seen how to use the test runner with some really simple (and throw-away) test cases; now, it's time to take a closer look at how we build test cases in PHPUnit.

At the highest level, you have a file containing a class extending off of one of the basic test classes. Remember your first basic test case example?

```php
1. <?php
2.
3. declare(strict_types=1);
4.
5. class BasicTestCase extends PHPUnit\Framework\TestCase
6. {
7.     public function testCase()
8.     {
9.         $this->assertTrue(false);
10.    }
11. }
```

To create test cases, you create class methods which need to be identified as tests. There are two ways to do this. You either prepend a test method with the word test like in your example, or you create a documentation block to the test method and add a @test annotation to indicate the method below is a test case. It looks like this:

```php
1. <?php
2.
3. declare(strict_types=1);
4.
5. class BasicTestCase extends PHPUnit\Framework\TestCase
6. {
7.     /**
8.      * @test
9.      */
10.    public function firstTestCase()
11.    {
12.        $this->assertTrue(False);
13.    }
14. }
```

What you name the test case when it's annotated doesn't really matter, but it's certainly better to be as descriptive as you can. When you execute this test with the test runner, the output looks similar to the following:

```
> phpunit BasicTestCase.php
PHPUnit 8.3.4 by Sebastian Bergmann and contributors.

F                                                              1 / 1
(100%)

Time: 108 ms, Memory: 12.00 MB

There was 1 failure:

1) BasicTestCase::firstTestCase
Failed asserting that false is true.

/Users/chartjes/grumpy-guide/test/basic_test_case.php:12

FAILURES!
Tests: 1, Assertions: 1, Failures: 1.
```

Pretty much the same output, but the test case that failed has a much more "human-friendly" name attached to it. Never forget that at the highest level, tests are really about people, and anything we do that makes it harder for people to use and understand the tests will cause friction and possibly lead to bad outcomes.

So why do you need to either annotate methods or prepend class method names with test? It's so the test runner can identify what methods are really tests, and what can be ignored because they might be helper methods you've created or setup and/or teardown methods that need to be executed.

What happens if you remove the annotation from our test case?

```php
1.  <?php
2.
3.  declare(strict_types=1);
4.
5.  class BasicTestCase extends PHPUnit\Framework\TestCase
6.  {
7.      public function firstTestCase()
8.      {
9.          $this->assertTrue(False);
10.     }
11. }
```

The test runner tells you…

```
PHPUnit 8.3.4 by Sebastian Bergmann and contributors.

W                                                             1 / 1
(100%)

Time: 109 ms, Memory: 12.00 MB

There was 1 warning:

1) Warning
No tests found in class "BasicTestCase".

WARNINGS!
Tests: 1, Assertions: 0, Warnings: 1.
```

…it did not find any tests. If you ever find yourself scratching your head as to why PHPUnit didn't find our test, the first place to look is at the names of your test methods and if you are using annotations or not.

I have covered the basics of how PHPUnit works. In the next chapter, I will show you a test design pattern I like to use to organize my tests to provide clarity and keep me focused on what I'm doing.

Chapter

5

Test Double

What Is a Test Double?

Test doubles are a concept that generates the most arguments between people discussing testing. They are a concept you have to understand to really have an opinion on them, but we all know that never stops people from arguing.

Wikipedia has a definition that gets right to the heart of the matter:

> *"In automated unit testing, it may be necessary to use objects or procedures that look and behave like their release-intended counterparts, but are actually simplified versions that reduce the complexity and facilitate testing. A test double is a generic (meta) term used for these objects or procedures."*

Test doubles are a tool we can use to represent dependencies we need for a given testing scenario. In the PHP world, they are commonly referred to as mocks, but I want to get you into the habit of using the correct word for it. You'll see why in a little bit.

At a high level, I will use a double to represent some dependency I need for a test when, for whatever reason, I am not using the real thing. There can be lots of reasons not to use the "real" dependency. The most common reasons are "it talks to a database" or "it talks to a remote API."

Before I go further, I want to be clear there are no right or wrong approaches to using test doubles. Some programming communities advocate using doubles for all dependencies. Some advocate never using a double. Other programming communities that use languages where objects and functions can be modified at run time (commonly referred to as "monkey patching") use that technique instead of doubles.

In this chapter, I want to show you the different types of test doubles available to PHP programmers and let you make up your own mind. My approach is to use the real dependency when possible unless there is significant overhead. Dependencies that use a database are the usual culprit for me or "request" objects used in frameworks.

In this chapter, I will be using the test doubling framework Prophecy[1], which has been available in PHPUnit since version 4.5. I've also used Mockery[2] and liked its syntax, too. There is no "right" one to use — you can even use PHPUnit's built-in test doubling tools. Pick one you like and stick with it; those who have to maintain the tests after you will thank you for being consistent.

In these examples, I will be using code that is being used in production for an application that helps track transactions in a simulation baseball league.

Dummies

Dummies are the first test double you might need. With Wikipedia as our guide:

> *"..used when a parameter is needed for the tested method but without actually needing to use the parameter."*

In practical use, you will want to use a dummy when the code you are testing needs a dependency, but the dependency itself will never be used during the test. With PHP moving towards type hints and return types being used more and more, dummies are of limited use

---

[1] Prophecy: https://github.com/phpspec/prophecy
[2] Mockery: https://github.com/mockery/mockery

because creating a dependency without a type will likely cause PHP to complain. If you are using older codebases where types are not being used, you can create a dummy by using PHP's built-in stdClass object.

So let's say you are writing a test that needs to use this particular bit of code:

```
1. class Roster
2. {
3.    public $_db;
4.    public $pdo;
5.    public $previous_season;
6.    public $current_season;
7.
8.    /**
9.     * Constructor for class
10.    *
11.    * @param Aura\SqlQuery\QueryFactory $db
12.    */
13.   public function __construct($db)
14.   {
15.      $this->_db = $db;
16.      $this->pdo = new PDO(
17.        'pgsql:host=localhost;dbname=;user=;password=');
18.   }
19.
20.   // Other code snipped out
21. }
```

But your test doesn't need to do anything with it. You'd be okay creating a dummy without a type to satisfy the condition of needing "a RosterModel object."

```
// Create a dummy of our database and pass it to our Roster model
$db = new stdClass();
$rm = new Roster($db);
```

Test Stub

In our world of typed PHP code, the dummy will get upgraded to the test stub. Again, using Wikipedia as our guide, we get the following definition:

> " used for providing the tested code with 'indirect input.'"

This is a shorter way of saying an object with the same class signature as our dependency but with no expectations that any methods of that object will be called during the test.

So, using the same code you're trying to test, but now you are type-hinting on what the $db parameter is supposed to be, so you need to create that as a test stub. This time you are using Prophecy to do so.

```
// Create a stub of the QueryFactory object the constructor needs
$db = $this->prophesize(QueryFactory::class);
$db->reveal();
$rm = new Roster($db);
```

In more clear language, what these two lines do is:

- Create a test double object with the same class signature as a QueryFactory (so it is of the correct type)
- Activate the double
- Create a Roster object that accepts our test double as a constructor parameter

Mock Objects and Test Spies

In this section, I am going to combine two types of test doubles because they are both going to be used in this test scenario.

First, we have a mock object which is used for verifying "indirect output" of the tested code by first defining the expectations before the tested code is executed.

A mock is the most common test double you will be using in your tests when you need a test double. Mocks are where we end up with very large amounts of code that is part of our arrange step.

Second, we have a test spy, used for verifying "indirect output" of the tested code, by asserting the expectations afterward, without having defined the expectations before the tested code is executed. It helps in recording information about the indirect object created.

Spies are used when you are expecting a method on a mock is going to be called, but you don't need to worry about any side effects (meaning actions the code in question takes) that happen.

In this example, you're writing a test for some code that generates entries in our "transaction log." This is code I have broken multiple times because I did not initially write tests for it. After some refactoring, here is the code you are going to test:

```
1. <?php
2. use Roster;
3.
4. class Transaction
5. {
6.     protected $rosterModel;
7.
8.     public function __construct(Roster $rosterModel)
9.     {
10.         $this->rosterModel = $rosterModel;
11.     }
12.
13.     public function generateTradeLogEntry($data, $tradePartner): string
14.     {
15.         $tradeDate = date('m/y');
16.         $tradedPlayers = [];
17.
18.         foreach ($data as $playerInfo) {
19.             [$tmp, $playerId] = explode('_', $playerInfo);
20.             $playerInfo = $this->rosterModel->getById($playerId);
21.             $comment = "Trade {$tradePartner} {$tradeDate}";
22.             if ($playerInfo['ibl_team'] !== $tradePartner) {
23.                 $tradedPlayers[] = trim($playerInfo['display_name']);
24.                 $this->rosterModel
25.                     ->updatePlayerTeam($tradePartner, $playerId, $comment);
26.                 $this->rosterModel->makeInactive($playerId);
27.             }
28.         }
29.
30.         return 'Trades ' . implode(', ', $tradedPlayers) . ' to ' . $tradePartner;
31.     }
32. }
```

So the first step is to identify dependencies. You have:

- A date that we cannot override (maybe refactor that later to avoid weird edge cases)
- A Roster object that calls getById()
- A Roster object that calls updatePlayerTeam()
- A Roster object that calls makeInactive()

What is your test scenario? First, you build a test skeleton with the scenario in it.

5. Test Double

```php
1. <?php
2. declare(strict_types=1);
3. use Aura\SqlQuery\QueryFactory;
4.
5. require __DIR__ . '/../models/rosters.php';
6. require __DIR__ . '/../models/transactions.php';
7.
8. class TransactionsTests extends PHPUnit\Framework\TestCase
9. {
10.    /**
11.     * @test
12.     */
13.    public function it_generates_proper_transaction_info_for_a_trade(): void
14.    {
15.      /**
16.       * Given I have an array that contains players
17.       * When I submit a list of players
18.       * And I submit a transaction description
19.       * Then I should get a one-line transaction being generated
20.       */
21.
22.      // Assert
23.      $this->assertTrue(false);
24.    }
25. }
```

Time to create the data you need for the test and a mock of the Roster object and then run your test. Remember to do this after every change to help you isolate any problems you run into!

```php
1. // Arrange
2. $expected = 'Trades Moe, Larry, Curly to TEST';
3. $tradePartner = 'TEST';
4.
5. // Data contains compound ID's of <trade partner 1>_<player_id>
6. $data = ['team1_1', 'team1_2', 'team1_3'];
7.
8. $rm = $this->prophesize(Roster::class);
9. $tm = new Transaction($rm->reveal());
```

The test fails (as it should!)

```
TypeError : Return value of Double\Roster\P1::getById() must be of the type
array, null returned
```

Now go back and implement the expected calls and return values on your mock. First, the getById() calls:

```
$rm->getById(1)
    ->willReturn(['ibl_team' => 'TEST', 'display_name' => 'Moe']);
$rm->getById(2)
    ->willReturn(['ibl_team' => 'TEST', 'display_name'=> 'Larry']);
$rm->getById(3)
    ->willReturn(['ibl_team' => 'TEST', 'display_name'=> 'Curly']);
```

Prophecy uses an API for mocks where you specify the method you are expecting to be called and then specify what will be returned by that specific call. Prophecy allows you to mock out multiple calls so you can have the exact level of control you need.

The test run fails…

```
Prophecy\Exception\Call\UnexpectedCallException : Unexpected method call on
Double\Roster\P1:
  - updatePlayerTeam(
      "TESTMORE",
      "1",
      "Trade TESTMORE 01/01"
  )
expected calls were:
  - getById(
      exact(1)
  )
  - getById(
      exact(2)
  )
  - getById(
      exact(3)
  )
```

… because you have not implemented the updatePlayerTeam() test spies.

Next, we have to create the expectations for the call to updatePlayerTeam(). There is a potential problem here. The updatePlayerTeam() method relies on passing in a date formatted in the way that it expected it, but we can't override it for testing purposes. This could lead to edge cases if the test happens to be run when the date rolls over from one day to the other. "This isn't a big deal, Chris," I can hear you saying. I prefer to have code that does not have this weird edge case. So, I ask you to refactor the Transaction model to have a tradeDate parameter that we set in the constructor but can override in the test.

```php
1. <?php
2.
3. class Transaction
4. {
5.     protected $rosterModel;
6.     public $transactionDate;
7.
8.     public function __construct(Roster $rosterModel)
9.     {
10.         $this->rosterModel = $rosterModel;
11.         $this->transactionDate = date('m/y');
12.     }
13.
14.     public function generateTradeLogEntry($data, $tradePartner): string
15.     {
16.         $tradedPlayers = [];
17.
18.         foreach ($data as $playerInfo) {
19.             [$tmp, $playerId] = explode('_', $playerInfo);
20.             $playerInfo = $this->rosterModel->getById($playerId);
21.             $comment = "Trade {$tradePartner} {$this->transactionDate}";
22.             if ($playerInfo['ibl_team'] !== $tradePartner) {
23.                 $tradedPlayers[] = trim($playerInfo['display_name']);
24.                 $this->rosterModel
25.                     ->updatePlayerTeam($tradePartner, $playerId, $comment);
26.                 $this->rosterModel
27.                     ->makeInactive($playerId);
28.             }
29.         }
30.
31.         return 'Trades ' . implode(', ', $tradedPlayers) . ' to ' . $tradePartner;
32.     }
33. }
```

Then, you set the transaction date to be whatever you want it to be for the purposes of the test:

```php
$tm = new Transaction($rm->reveal());
$tm->transactionDate = '01/01';
```

Next, you create your test spies with specific calls you are expecting to happen:

```
// Create our updatePlayerTeam test spies
$rm->updatePlayerTeam($tradePartner, 1, $tradeComment)->shouldBeCalled();
$rm->updatePlayerTeam($tradePartner, 2, $tradeComment)->shouldBeCalled();
$rm->updatePlayerTeam($tradePartner, 3, $tradeComment)->shouldBeCalled();
```

Those of you who sneak a peek at the documentation for Prophecy will note there are ways to create these spies without being specific about what parameters and in what order they go in. I could've done the spies like this:

```
// Create our updatePlayerTeam test spies
$rm->updatePlayerTeam(
    \Prophecy\Argument::any(),
    \Prophecy\Argument::any(),
    \Prophecy\Argument::any())
    ->shouldBeCalled(3);
```

Which translates to "I expect updatePlayerTeam() to be called, with any values as three arguments, three times." I prefer for my tests to be as specific as possible, as it reduces the likelihood of a test case failing in a way I did not expect.

The test fails…

```
Prophecy\Exception\Call\UnexpectedCallException : Unexpected method call on
Double\Roster\P1:
  - makeInactive(
      "1"
  )
expected calls were:
  - getById(
      exact(1)
  )
  - getById(
      exact(2)
  )
  - getById(
      exact(3)
  )
  - updatePlayerTeam(
      exact("TESTMORE"),
      exact(1),
      exact("Trade TESTMORE 01/01")
  )
```

```
    - updatePlayerTeam(
        exact("TESTMORE"),
        exact(2),
        exact("Trade TESTMORE 01/01")
    )
    - updatePlayerTeam(
        exact("TESTMORE"),
        exact(3),
        exact("Trade TESTMORE 01/01")
    )
```

… because you have one more set of test spies to implement. You can follow the same pattern for the makeInactive() call as you did for updatePlayerTeam().

```
$rm->makeInactive(1)->shouldBeCalled();
$rm->makeInactive(2)->shouldBeCalled();
$rm->makeInactive(3)->shouldBeCalled();
```

Now you have a test that passes!

```
OK (1 test, 7 assertions)
```

One more refactor to not hard-code values in your dependencies so changes happen in one place (in this case for the player IDs), and here is the completed test.

```php
 1. <?php
 2. declare(strict_types=1);
 3.
 4. require __DIR__ . '/../models/rosters.php';
 5. require __DIR__ . '/../models/transactions.php';
 6.
 7. class TransactionsTests extends PHPUnit\Framework\TestCase
 8. {
 9.     /**
10.      * @test
11.      */
12.     public function it_generates_proper_transaction_info_for_a_trade(): void
13.     {
14.         /**
15.          * Given I have an array that contains players
16.          * When I submit a list of players
17.          * And I submit a transaction description
18.          * Then I should get a one-line transaction being generated
19.          */
20.         // Arrange
```

```
21.          $expected = 'Trades Moe, Larry, Curly to TESTMORE';
22.          $tradePartner = 'TESTMORE';
23.          $tradeComment = 'Trade TESTMORE 01/01';
24.
25.          // Data contains compound ID's of <trade partner 1>_<player_id>
26.          $data = ['team1_1', 'team1_2', 'team1_3'];
27.          $rm = $this->prophesize(Roster::class);
28.          $playerIds = [1, 2, 3];
29.
30.          // Mock our getById() calls
31.          $rm->getById($playerIds[0])->willReturn(
32.            ['ibl_team' => 'TEST',
33.             'display_name' => 'Moe']);
34.          $rm->getById($playerIds[1])->willReturn(
35.            ['ibl_team' => 'TEST',
36.             'display_name'=> 'Larry']);
37.          $rm->getById($playerIds[2])->willReturn(
38.            ['ibl_team' => 'TEST',
39.             'display_name'=> 'Curly']);
40.
41.          // Create our updatePlayerTeam test spies
42.          $rm->updatePlayerTeam(
43.            $tradePartner,
44.            $playerIds[0],
45.            $tradeComment)->shouldBeCalled();
46.          $rm->updatePlayerTeam(
47.            $tradePartner,
48.            $playerIds[1],
49.            $tradeComment)->shouldBeCalled();
50.          $rm->updatePlayerTeam(
51.            $tradePartner,
52.            $playerIds[2],
53.            $tradeComment)->shouldBeCalled();
54.
55.          $rm->makeInactive($playerIds[0])->shouldBeCalled();
56.          $rm->makeInactive($playerIds[1])->shouldBeCalled();
57.          $rm->makeInactive($playerIds[2])->shouldBeCalled();
58.
59.          $tm = new Transaction($rm->reveal());
60.          $tm->transactionDate = '01/01';
61.
62.          // Act
63.          $response = $tm->generateTradeLogEntry(
64.            $data, $tradePartner);
65.
```

```
66.        // Assert
67.        $this->assertEquals($expected, $response);
68.    }
69. }
```

Fakes

Fakes are an often under-utilized tool for testing purposes. Instead of using a mock created with the testing frameworks tools, you instead create your own object that does the same thing you are expecting from your dependency. Using the example of the test we just wrote above, what would it look like if I decided I wanted to use a fake instead of what Prophecy can provide me.

There are a few ways you can approach this. You could create a standalone object outside of the test that extends the methods we are creating doubles for. That might look like this:

```php
1. <?php
2. declare(strict_types=1);
3.
4. class FakeRosterModel
5. {
6.     public function getById($id): array
7.     {
8.         $responses = [
9.             0 => ['ibl_team' => 'TEST', 'display_name' => 'Moe'],
10.            1 => ['ibl_team' => 'TEST', 'display_name'=> 'Larry'],
11.            2 => ['ibl_team' => 'TEST', 'display_name'=> 'Curly'],
12.        ];
13.
14.        return $responses[$id];
15.    }
16.
17.    public function updatePlayerTeam(
18.      $iblTeam, $playerId, $comments = ''): bool
19.    {
20.        return true;
21.    }
22.
23.    public function makeInactive($player_id): bool
24.    {
25.        return true;
26.    }
27. }
```

The big issue is the Transaction object is expecting a typed Roster object in the constructor. There is no easy way to fix this. I could extend this object from Roster and pass it a QueryFactory but do nothing with it. That seems like the path of least resistance if I really wanted to use a fake instead of Prophecy for the Roster object. So I will do that. The fake now looks like this:

```php
1.  <?php
2.  declare(strict_types=1);
3.
4.  require_once __DIR__ . '/../models/rosters.php';
5.
6.  class FakeRosterModel extends Roster
7.  {
8.      public function __construct($db)
9.      {
10.         $this->db = $db;
11.     }
12.
13.     public function getById($id): array
14.     {
15.         $responses = [
16.             1 => ['ibl_team' => 'TEST', 'display_name' => 'Moe'],
17.             2 => ['ibl_team' => 'TEST', 'display_name'=> 'Larry'],
18.             3 => ['ibl_team' => 'TEST', 'display_name'=> 'Curly'],
19.         ];
20.
21.         return $responses[$id];
22.     }
23.
24.     public function updatePlayerTeam(
25.       $iblTeam, $playerId, $comments = ''): bool
26.     {
27.         return true;
28.     }
29.
30.     public function makeInactive($player_id): bool
31.     {
32.         return true;
33.     }
34. }
```

And my test using the fake looks like this:

```
1.  /**
2.   * @test
3.   */
4.  public function it_generates_proper_transaction_info_for_a_trade_using_fakes(): void
5.  {
6.      /**
7.       * Given I have an array that contains players
8.       * When I submit a list of players
9.       * And I submit a transaction description
10.      * Then I should get a one-line transaction being generated
11.      */
12.     // Arrange
13.     $expected = 'Trades Moe, Larry, Curly to TESTMORE';
14.     $tradePartner = 'TESTMORE';
15.
16.     // Data contains compound ID's of <trade partner 1>_<player_id>
17.     $data = ['team1_1', 'team1_2', 'team1_3'];
18.
19.     $rm = new FakeRosterModel(new \Aura\SqlQuery\QueryFactory('sqlite'));
20.     $tm = new Transaction($rm);
21.     $tm->transactionDate = '01/01';
22.
23.     // Act
24.     $response = $tm->generateTradeLogEntry($data, $tradePartner);
25.
26.     // Assert
27.     $this->assertEquals($expected, $response);
28. }
```

Or, I could create that fake inside our test by using the anonymous classes features available in more recent versions of PHP. This is what the test case would look like:

```
1.  /**
2.   * @test
3.   */
4.  public function it_generates_proper_transaction_info_for_a_trade_using_fakes(): void
5.  {
6.      /**
7.       * Given I have an array that contains players
8.       * When I submit a list of players
9.       * And I submit a transaction description
10.      * Then I should get a one-line transaction being generated
11.      */
```

```
12.    // Arrange
13.    $expected = 'Trades Moe, Larry, Curly to TESTMORE';
14.    $tradePartner = 'TESTMORE';
15.
16.    // Data contains compound ID's of <trade partner 1>_<player_id>
17.    $data = ['team1_1', 'team1_2', 'team1_3'];
18.    $db = new \Aura\SqlQuery\QueryFactory('sqlite');
19.
20.    $rm = new class($db) extends Roster  {
21.        public function __construct(\Aura\SqlQuery\QueryFactory $db)
22.        {
23.            $this->db = $db;
24.        }
25.        public function getById($id): array
26.        {
27.            $responses = [
28.                1 => ['ibl_team' => 'TEST', 'display_name' => 'Moe'],
29.                2 => ['ibl_team' => 'TEST', 'display_name'=> 'Larry'],
30.                3 => ['ibl_team' => 'TEST', 'display_name'=> 'Curly'],
31.            ];
32.            return $responses[$id];
33.        }
34.        public function updatePlayerTeam($iblTeam, $playerId, $comments = ''): bool
35.        {
36.            return true;
37.        }
38.        public function makeInactive($player_id): bool
39.        {
40.            return true;
41.        }
42.    };
43.    $tm = new Transaction($rm);
44.    $tm->transactionDate = '01/01';
45.
46.    // Act
47.    $response = $tm->generateTradeLogEntry($data, $tradePartner);
48.
49.    // Assert
50.    $this->assertEquals($expected, $response);
51. }
```

Whatever path you decide to go, it is good to know you can create a double of something that perhaps is a lot of work to duplicate using test doubling tools. Think about things that send emails when you do not want emails to be sent at all as part of the test. You can create a fake object that uses all the same methods but never sends it.

My preference when it comes to fakes is to use anonymous classes in the test cases unless you are 100% sure the fake you are creating can be reused by other tests. Remember, the same rules about reusing code and trying not to repeat yourself apply to your tests!

Final Thoughts

Tests are all about scenarios where you control the state of all your dependencies. Sometimes you can use the "real" dependency–other times you will need to create a double. You have multiple doubles to choose, depending on what you need:

- Dummies if you're not using type-hinted code and need a dependency that you're not going to be calling any methods on in your test

- Test stubs if you need a dummy, but your code is type-hinted

- Spies if you need a stub where some methods are going to be called, but you don't need to worry if the method does anything

- Mocks if you need a dependency with specific methods being called and those methods need to return something or perform an action required by the test

Tests doubles are definitely the number one thing testing practitioners argue about—the next being how many assertions should be in each test. This chapter should give you the confidence to determine when test doubles are appropriate and which ones to choose.

Chapter 6

Test-Driven Development by Example

In an idealized world of software development, you would be writing all the code for your applications using Test-Driven Development (TDD), implementing features, and deciding on APIs and interfaces one test at a time. The way I use TDD follows this type of workflow:

- Create an empty test that fails
- Write out my testing scenario as pseudocode
- Turn the pseudocode into a PHPUnit test
- Run the test
- If it fails, keep writing code until the behavior I am testing passes

My experiences over the years have been that a lot of programmers can benefit from both the structure and the discipline that TDD forces upon you. I like how focusing on one test at a time keeps my mind from wandering and thinking too far ahead. Of course, I am always thinking about what I am doing from a high level, but I work very hard to implement the simplest solution to make the test pass, knowing I can use the test to verify I do not break anything when I go back and refactor the code.

In this example, I'm going to be solving the following problem:

> *Write some code that takes any Arabic number and turns it into its Roman numeral equivalent for any number up to 100.*

This is a good problem because it is one that has a known solution (easier to write tests for) and requires you to have a good grasp of several common programming techniques and structures.

Tooling

I worked on these examples on my late 2016 MacBook Pro laptop, running macOS 10.14.6. I use PhpStorm (with Vim bindings enabled because I am a supporter of the One True Editor) to write my PHP code. I am using PHP 7.3.6 installed using Homebrew and have installed the PHAR version of PHPUnit as per the instructions on the PHPUnit website.

The specifics of what I am using don't really matter! You don't have to copy what I am doing to write tests. Just make sure you have a stable version of PHP installed and PHPUnit available to you.

Getting Started

I've created an empty directory to put my code in. I will have my code in the src directory and my tests in the tests directory. Due to PHP and PHPUnit's flexibility, you can organize these things whatever way you want as long as you handle your paths correctly.

First, let's talk about how to solve this problem. Roman numerals consist of creating a string consisting of symbols that together represent positive Arabic integer values. You read the result from left to right. So what are the base symbols we need to worry about?

- I -> 1
- V -> 5
- X -> 10

- L -> 50
- C -> 100

There are some numbers that are presented in a different way, so we need to account for those as well:

- IV -> 4
- IX -> 9

So, let's create an empty test that would verify that when we pass in 1, we get back I.

```php
1. <?php
2. declare(strict_types=1);
3.
4. class NumeralConverterTest extends PHPUnit\Framework\TestCase
5. {
6.     /**
7.      * @test
8.      */
9.     public function converts1ToRomanNumeral() : void
10.    {
11.        $this->assertTrue(false);
12.    }
13. }
```

This is the bare minimum test class that will run without PHP or PHPUnit complaining we have not configured things correctly.

I like to use the @test annotation in the document block for my tests instead of prepending every test method with test. It allows me to create test method names that are closer to how I would describe the test in English.

If I run this test, it fails:

```
Failed asserting that false is true.
 /Users/chartjes/grumpy-guide/test/NumeralConverterTest.php:11



Time: 188 ms, Memory: 12.00 MB
```

First Test

The first test is always the hardest because we are setting the stage for all the other code that comes afterward. I definitely spend some time prototyping or thinking about what I want my interfaces and parameters to look like. In this case, I have a pretty good idea from the start what I want things to look like. I will write the first test case:

```
1. public function converts1ToRomanNumeral() : void
2. {
3.     // Arrange
4.     $nc = new NumeralConverter();
5.     $input = 1;
6.     $output = 'I';
7.
8.     // Act
9.     $result = $nc->arabicToRoman($input);
10.
11.    // Assert
12.    $this->assertEquals($output, $result);
13. }
```

Before we get into the specifics, I want to talk about a test design pattern taught to me many years ago that I use on a regular basis to keep my test cases organized. It's called the Arrange-Act-Assert pattern.

Arrange

This section is where I create any dependencies I need for the testing scenario. In this example, I am creating a NumeralConvertor object along with my input for the method and the expected output. In more advanced test cases, the code I need to create test doubles would go in the arrange section as well. In most test cases, the arrange step contains the most code.

Act

This is where we use the code we are testing to generate output we can then verify matches our expectations. In our example, we are executing the arabicToRoman() method, passing our selected input in and storing the output in a variable.

This section can contain a lot of code or maybe just one line, like in our example. It really depends on the testing scenario. One thing to look out for is making sure that whatever is going on in the section follows what is going on in the application code that uses whatever we are testing. The further you drift away from using the code in your tests from how it is used in production, the more likely you will end up with tests that pass but applications that do not work as expected.

Assert

The final section of the test is the one where we have all our assertions or other statements that verify our code is behaving the way we expect. Some people follow a rule of "one assertion per test," while others follow "use however many assertions you need." There is no correct answer, but a test case without some kind of assertion is not testing anything. In our example, we are verifying the expected output matches what the `arabicToRoman()` method returns.

Back to our example; it fails because I haven't created my `NumeralConvertor` object.

```
Error : Class 'NumeralConverter' not found
  /Users/chartjes/grumpy-guide/test/NumeralConverterTest.php:11
```

Let me create an empty shell for the object.

```php
<?php
declare(strict_types=1);

class NumeralConverter
{

}
```

Then, I update my test by adding a line where to load this object:

```php
require __DIR__ . '/../src/NumeralConverter.php';
```

Finally, I run the test again, and it fails because the method I am testing doesn't exist yet.

```
Error : Call to undefined method NumeralConverter::arabicToRoman()
  /Users/chartjes/grumpy-guide/test/NumeralConverterTest.php:16
```

Yes, this is exactly how I do my testing work. I go slow and steady, making sure not to leave anything out. We all have our own habits and programming techniques we like to use; being deliberate minimizes the likelihood I skip steps and make an easily avoidable mistake.

Now I write just enough code to satisfy the behavior we are testing for.

```
 1. public function arabicToRoman($value) : string
 2. {
 3.     $result = '';
 4.
 5.     if ($value === 1) {
 6.         $result .= 'I';
 7.     }
 8.
 9.     return $result;
10. }
```

The test passes.

```
OK (1 test, 1 assertion)
```

Next Test

Of course, my solution is very simplistic and makes a bunch of assumptions that are going to clearly change. Rather than go ahead and try and build an optimal solution from the beginning, I decided to think clearly about what I want to do. For the next test, which is verifying that we handle converting 2 and 3 (I decided to group them together), I am going to introduce the concept of the data provider.

A data provider is a method that passes in data sets to a test method. In implementation, it is a method that returns an array of arrays. I am going to start off by creating the data provider method. The naming convention doesn't matter–try and create something that is verbose and conveys meaning to others who will have to read the test code.

```
public function dataSetsForConversion() : array
{
    return [
        [2, 'II'],
        [3, 'III']
    ];
}
```

Then, I create a failing test method that uses the data provider.

```
/**
 * @dataProvider  dataSetsForConversion
 * @test
 */
public function converts2and3ToRomanNumeral($input, $expected)
{
    $this->assertTrue(false);
}
```

To tell PHPUnit what data provider to use for a test case, you need to have a DocBlock (if you aren't using one already) for the test method and then add the @dataProvider annotation to it. Case matters! Then, you need to have your test method accept as many parameters as individual data values you are passing in.

For this test, I decided to provide the input I am testing and what I expect the results to be.

Now I verify that the test fails.

```
Failed asserting that false is true.
 /Users/chartjes/grumpy-guide/test/NumeralConverterTest.php:34



Failed asserting that false is true.
 /Users/chartjes/grumpy-guide/test/NumeralConverterTest.php:34
```

No, I didn't cut-and-paste the result twice. The test method using this provider is executed once for each data set.

With the first step done, I go and start implementing code to make this second test case pass.

```
 1. public function arabicToRoman($value) : string
 2. {
 3.     $currentValue = $value;
 4.     $result = '';
 5.
 6.     while ($currentValue > 0) {
 7.         if ($currentValue % 1 === 0) {
 8.             $result .= 'I';
 9.             $currentValue--;
10.         }
11.     }
12.
13.     return $result;
14. }
```

The test passes.

Building Further Test Cases

The implementation I did for the test case that proves 2 and 3 are converted correctly has me feeling like I should just continue to extend my code to handle other situations in a similar way. I'll add a test case which verifies 4, 5, and 9 are handled correctly. These represent behavior that is outside the norm.

First, the failing test.

```php
/**
 * @dataProvider exceptionDataSets
 * @test
 */
public function convertsSingleDigitExceptions($input, $expected)
{
    $this->assertTrue(false);
}
```

It fails as I expect it to.

```
Failed asserting that false is true.
 /Users/chartjes/grumpy-guide/test/NumeralConverterTest.php:53


Failed asserting that false is true.
 /Users/chartjes/grumpy-guide/test/NumeralConverterTest.php:53


Failed asserting that false is true.
 /Users/chartjes/grumpy-guide/test/NumeralConverterTest.php:53
```

There are three failures because I'm using three data sets.

Then, I modify the code to handle this new behavior correctly.

```php
1. public function arabicToRoman($value) : string
2. {
3.     $currentValue = $value;
4.     $result = '';
5.
6.     while ($currentValue > 0) {
7.         switch ($currentValue) {
8.             case $currentValue % 9 === 0:
9.                 $result .= 'IX';
10.                $currentValue -= 9;
11.                break;
```

```
12.            case $currentValue % 5 === 0:
13.                $result .= 'V';
14.                $currentValue -= 5;
15.                break;
16.            case $currentValue % 4 === 0:
17.                $result .= 'IV';
18.                $currentValue -= 4;
19.                break;
20.            case $currentValue % 1 === 0:
21.                $result .= 'I';
22.                $currentValue--;
23.                break;
24.        }
25.    }
26.
27.    return $result;
28. }
```

The tests pass.

```
OK (3 tests, 3 assertions)
```

As a final check, let me make sure the entire test suite passes.

```
OK (6 tests, 6 assertions)
```

Refactoring The Tests

Looking at the tests I have written, I notice I have been duplicating some data providers. I should probably just put all the data I am using for the tests into one data provider. That also means I only need one test method.

The new data provider looks like this:

```
1. public function dataSetsForConversion() : array
2. {
3.    return [
4.        [1, 'I'],
5.        [2, 'II'],
6.        [3, 'III'],
7.        [4, 'IV'],
8.        [5, 'V'],
9.        [9, 'IX']
10.    ];
11. }
```

I can reuse an existing test:

```
1. /**
2.  * @dataProvider  dataSetsForConversion
3.  * @test
4.  */
5. public function convertsArabicToRoman($input, $expected)
6. {
7.     $nc = new NumeralConverter();
8.     $this->assertEquals($expected, $nc->arabicToRoman($input));
9. }
```

Everything still passes.

```
OK (6 tests, 6 assertions)
```

Now, I add some more data sets to handle converting 10, 50, and 100 correctly.

```
1. return [
2.     [1, 'I'],
3.     [2, 'II'],
4.     [3, 'III'],
5.     [4, 'IV'],
6.     [5, 'V'],
7.     [9, 'IX'],
8.     [10, 'X'],
9.     [50, 'L'],
10.    [100, 'C']
11. ];
```

Run the tests to make sure things pass.

```
Failed asserting that two strings are equal.
Expected :'X'
Actual   :'VV'
 /Users/chartjes/grumpy-guide/test/NumeralConverterTest.php:30


Failed asserting that two strings are equal.
Expected :'L'
Actual   :'VIXIXIXIXIX'
 /Users/chartjes/grumpy-guide/test/NumeralConverterTest.php:30


Failed asserting that two strings are equal.
Expected :'C'
Actual   :'VVIXIXIXIXIXIXIXIXIXIX'
 /Users/chartjes/grumpy-guide/test/NumeralConverterTest.php:30
```

Wait! What happened? Aha, I forgot to add in code to handle these values correctly. Let me do that now.

```
1. case $currentValue % 100 === 0:
2.     $result .= 'C';
3.     $currentValue -= 100;
4.     break;
5. case $currentValue % 50 === 0:
6.     $result .= 'L';
7.     $currentValue -= 50;
8.     break;
9. case $currentValue % 10 === 0:
10.    $result .= 'X';
11.    $currentValue -= 10;
12.    break;
```

Now the tests pass.

```
OK (9 tests, 9 assertions)
```

Now, I go to the Wikipedia page for Roman numerals and add some values in the data set, refactoring them to have them in numeric order:

```
1. return [
2.     [1, 'I'],
3.     [2, 'II'],
4.     [3, 'III'],
5.     [4, 'IV'],
6.     [5, 'V'],
7.     [9, 'IX'],
8.     [10, 'X'],
9.     [14, 'XIV'],
10.    [15, 'XV'],
11.    [29, 'XXIV'],
12.    [40, 'XL'],
13.    [44, 'XLIV'],
14.    [49, 'XXXXIX'],
15.    [50, 'L'],
16.    [57, 'LVII'],
17.    [63, 'LXIII'],
18.    [78, 'LXXVII'],
19.    [82, 'LXXXII'],
20.    [91, 'XCI'],
21.    [100, 'C']
22. ];
```

I run the tests.

```
Failed asserting that two strings are equal.
Expected :'XIV'
Actual   :'IIIVIVIV'

Failed asserting that two strings are equal.
Expected :'XV'
Actual   :'VX'

Failed asserting that two strings are equal.
Expected :'XXIV'
Actual   :'IIVIVXX'

Failed asserting that two strings are equal.
Expected :'XL'
Actual   :'XXXX'

Failed asserting that two strings are equal.
Expected :'XLIV'
Actual   :'IVXXXX'

Failed asserting that two strings are equal.
Expected :'XXXXIX'
Actual   :'IIVIVXXXX'

Failed asserting that two strings are equal.
Expected :'LVII'
Actual   :'IIVIVIVIVXXXX'

Failed asserting that two strings are equal.
Expected :'LXIII'
Actual   :'IXIXIXIXIXIXIX'

Failed asserting that two strings are equal.
Expected :'LXXVII'
Actual   :'IIIVIXIXIXIXIXIXIXIX'

Failed asserting that two strings are equal.
Expected :'LXXXII'
Actual   :'IIXIXIXIXIXIXIXIXIX'

Failed asserting that two strings are equal.
Expected :'XCI'
Actual   :'IXXXXL'

FAILURES!
Tests: 20, Assertions: 20, Failures: 11.
```

Ugh. Not again! See, I forgot to handle some of these exceptional values correctly, and I have mistakes in my data set. I go back through the error messages and the data set and fix them.

I have made a bunch of mistakes in my implementation (remember, I am actually doing this without cheating and looking on Stack Overflow or some other website full of answers I can cut-and-paste into my code).

This also illustrates why having the tests is so useful when you are forced to refactor code behind the scenes. Time to rethink how I am doing this!

Okay, so now I have correct values in my data provider, and I added one to make sure 6 gets handled correctly.

```
1.  return [
2.      [1, 'I'],
3.      [2, 'II'],
4.      [3, 'III'],
5.      [4, 'IV'],
6.      [5, 'V'],
7.      [9, 'IX'],
8.      [10, 'X'],
9.      [14, 'XIV'],
10.     [15, 'XV'],
11.     [29, 'XXIX'],
12.     [36, 'XXXVI'],
13.     [40, 'XL'],
14.     [44, 'XLIV'],
15.     [49, 'XLIX'],
16.     [50, 'L'],
17.     [57, 'LVII'],
18.     [63, 'LXIII'],
19.     [78, 'LXXVIII'],
20.     [82, 'LXXXII'],
21.     [91, 'XCI'],
22.     [100, 'C']
```

Here is the new implementation for the code that does the converting:

```
1.  while ($currentValue > 0) {
2.    switch ($currentValue) {
3.      case $currentValue - 100 >= 0:
4.        $result .= 'C';
5.        $currentValue -= 100;
6.        break;
7.      case $currentValue - 90 >= 0:
8.        $result .= 'XC';
9.        $currentValue -= 90;
10.       break;
11.     case $currentValue - 50 >= 0:
12.       $result .= 'L';
13.       $currentValue -= 50;
14.       break;
15.     case $currentValue - 40 >= 0:
16.       $result .= 'XL';
17.       $currentValue -= 40;
18.       break;
19.     case $currentValue - 10 >= 0:
20.       $result .= 'X';
21.       $currentValue -= 10;
22.       break;
23.     case $currentValue - 9 >= 0:
24.       $result .= 'IX';
25.       $currentValue -= 9;
26.       break;
27.     case $currentValue - 5 >= 0:
28.       $result .= 'V';
29.       $currentValue -= 5;
30.       break;
31.     case $currentValue - 4 >= 0:
32.       $result .= 'IV';
33.       $currentValue -= 4;
34.       break;
35.     case $currentValue - 1 >= 0:
36.       $result .= 'I';
37.       $currentValue--;
38.       break;
39.   }
```

Now all the tests pass!

```
OK (21 tests, 21 assertions)
```

Handling Non-Valid Input

Way back at the beginning of this chapter, I mentioned a few things in passing. First, we need to make sure we only accept integers. I've decided I will have the code throw exceptions when we encounter values outside what we are supposed to be converting.

Testing exceptions in PHPUnit 8.x is done with a few built-in methods (you can check them out in the documentation). I am going to use two of these methods. The first is `$this->expectException()` to verify the native PHP exception class is being thrown. The second one is `$this->expectExceptionMessage()`, to test that I get the messages I am expecting.

I start with a failing test to make sure we only except positive integers.

```
/**
 * @test
 */
public function onlyAcceptsPositiveIntegers()
{
    $this->assertTrue(false);
}
```

Then, I write the test using these helper methods to define what exceptions and messages I am supposed to be seeing.

```
public function onlyAcceptsPositiveIntegers()
{
    $this->expectException(RuntimeException::class);
    $this->expectExceptionMessage('This method converts positive integers only');
    $nc = new NumeralConverter();
    $nc->arabicToRoman(0);
}
```

The test should fail.

```
Failed asserting that exception of type "RuntimeException" is thrown.
```

Then, I write the code which implements the behavior I am expecting.

```
if (!(is_int($value) && $value > 0)) {
    throw new RuntimeException('This method converts positive integers only');
}
```

This test passes.

```
OK (1 test, 2 assertions)
```

The next test I add is one that makes sure we do not accept any values greater than 100. This is something we could remove later, but the original requirement (don't give in to scope creep!) is to only handle things up to 100.

Again, I start with a failing test.

```
/**
 * @test
 */
public function onlyAccepts100orLess()
{
    $this->assertTrue(false);
}
```

I write a test expecting a specific exception and exception message.

```
public function onlyAccepts100orLess()
{
    $this->expectException(RuntimeException::class);
    $this->expectExceptionMessage('This method converts positive integers less
than or equal to 100');
    $nc = new NumeralConverter();
    $nc->arabicToRoman(101);
}
```

Verify that this test fails.

```
Failed asserting that exception of type "RuntimeException" is thrown.
```

Write the code that implements this expected behavior.

```
if ($value > 100) {
    throw new RuntimeException('This method converts positive integers less than
or equal to 100');
}
```

This test passes.

```
OK (1 test, 2 assertions)
```

The entire test suite passes.

```
OK (23 tests, 25 assertions)
```

Final Thoughts

TDD does force you to do things differently than you are probably used to. It focuses on the code at a much lower level, making sure you don't move on to write other code once the code you have already written is behaving as expected. I think a good analogy for this is thinking of it as building code out of Lego blocks. One by one, you snap them together and, hopefully, the end result is what you expect it to be.

Chapter

7

Test-After Development by Example

What's the Difference?

The previous chapter where I showed you an example of using Test-Driven Development illustrated how much TDD is a design pattern with the side-effect of having tests that prove the code you wrote is behaving as expected. When you already have some code in place, and it's working to provide business value or otherwise solve a problem, you need to approach the process of testing it differently.

In these scenarios, I have found myself asking the same three questions over the years.

- What is the expected behavior?

- How am I going to test for that behavior?

- What am I going to have to change to test this code?

The biggest challenge for writing tests after we have working code is that the changes that need to be made in order for it "to be testable" can be challenging. It is very likely something will have to change. This fear of changing something that is "already working" is a real obstacle towards writing tests for existing code.

Because code is often written without any thought toward its testability in isolation, I find it very hard to offer anything more than generic advice. I do think examples of how to do this are very helpful. Lucky for us, I have one in mind.

What Is the Expected Behavior?

Many, many years ago, I wrote some web-based tools to help with the administration of the tabletop baseball league I am a member of. We needed something to manage the various transactions that occur: trades, player signings, and roster moves. The code was originally written in 2005 and, I'm sad to say, I did not write any tests for it. I needed it done in a hurry, so I slapped together a prototype with a very bad interface. The prototype became the production version. It has undergone some revisions over the years (drag-and-drop interfaces to make trades), but much of the code remains the same.

One of the parts of the application that has given me lots of problems is code that displays the "uncharted" status of a player. The league has rules about retaining players on your teams during seasons when they do not have a card representing them in the game that we use. We recently updated some of those rules, so I had to add code to make sure that whenever we were displaying details about a player, we were showing their "uncarded status" if it was applicable.

Each player has a row in a table in a Postgres database. There is a field indicating the "season" a player was uncharted. This is a two-digit integer–19 to represent 2019, for example. The display logic should be like this:

Given I am player And I had uncarded status for this season Or I had uncharted status for last season When my details are shown I should see my name And I should see my uncarded status

It seemed like almost every time I updated some part of the website to use the new behavior, I would manage to break it. The person who handles all the league transactions would message me to tell me, "It's not displaying uncarded status properly... again." So, it's time I wrote some tests to make sure I do not break this again.

I am going to show how I wrote tests for the existing code and the changes I made to the existing code in order to make it testable. There are two things I need to test: that players with uncarded statuses that need to be noted are displayed correctly and that any transactions involving players correctly includes any details about if the player is uncarded or not.

How Am I Going to Test This?

The first step is to find some code that talks to the database to get information about a player and make sure it is checking for uncarded status.

```
1.  public function getById($id)
2.  {
3.      $select = $this->_db->newSelect();
4.      $select->cols(['*'])
5.          ->from('rosters')
6.          ->where('id = :id')
7.          ->bindValue('id', $id);
8.      $sth = $this->pdo->prepare($select->getStatement());
9.      $sth->execute($select->getBindValues());
10.     $response = $sth->fetch(PDO::FETCH_ASSOC);
11.
12.     if (empty($response)) {
13.         return [];
14.     }
15.
16.     $response['display_name'] = trim($response['tig_name']);
17.
18.     if ($response['uncarded'] === $this->previous_season
19.         || $response['uncarded'] === $this->current_season) {
20.         $response['display_name'] .=
21.     ' [UC' . $response['uncarded'] . ']';
22.     }
23.
24.     return $response;
25. }
```

It seems like a good test is to create a scenario where we retrieve a record from the database that contains a player who has their uncarded status set to the current season. Then, I should check to make sure the resulting details are as we expect. Here is the outline of a test, written as if everything is working already. I'll go back and figure out dependencies later.

```php
1.  <?php
2.  require __DIR__ . '/../models/rosters.php';
3.
4.  class RostersTests extends PHPUnit\Framework\TestCase
5.  {
6.      /**
7.       * @test
8.       */
9.      public function it_displays_uncarded_players_correctly()
10.     {
11.         // Arrange
12.         require __DIR__ . '/../db_config.php';
13.         $rm = new Roster($db);
14.         $expected = 'TST McTesterton [UC19]';
15.
16.         // Act
17.         $response = $rm->getById(1);
18.
19.         // Assert
20.         $this->assertEquals($expected, $response['display_name']);
21.     }
22. }
```

This test fails because I don't have a player in the database with an ID of 1 that matches the expected player name. I need to create a double of the database connection that returns the information we're expecting to get. At this point in figuring out a test, we have two options.

I can go down the road of using real dependencies for this test or create doubles of everything that I need. When I look at the code itself, I need dependencies for:

- the database object
- a 'select' object that needs to be returned
- five different methods on the select object that need to be fluid
- a PDO object with a prepare method that returns a statement
- a PDO statement with two different methods

That is a lot of work to create doubles for. The arrange part of the test will be very big. If I don't want to do any of that, maybe I could create an in-memory database for this test? That way, I could insert the record I need, and then it goes away when the test is over. I'm not sure I want to create all those test doubles. I'll check the documentation for both PDO and the other SQL library I chose to use (Aura.sql) and see if I can do it in memory or with SQLite. The attributes that store the Aura object and the PDO object are set to public visibility so I could override them after I've created my Roster object.

This is what the test looks like now — note that I am only changing the way I am creating some of those dependencies, not the test itself.

```
1.  public function it_displays_uncarded_players_correctly()
2.  {
3.      // Arrange
4.      $db = new QueryFactory('sqlite');
5.      $pdo = new PDO('sqlite::memory:');
6.      $commands = [
7.          'CREATE TABLE IF NOT EXISTS rosters (
8.          id INTEGER PRIMARY KEY,
9.          tig_name TEXT,
10.         ibl_team TEXT,
11.         comments TEXT,
12.         status INTEGER,
13.         item_type INTEGER,
14.         uncarded INTEGER DEFAULT 0,
15.         retro_id TEXT)',
16.         "INSERT INTO rosters(tig_name, ibl_team, comments, status, item_type,
uncarded, retro_id)
17.         VALUES('TST McTesterton', 'TST', 'Test player', 1, 1, 19, 'retroid')"
18.     ];
19.     foreach ($commands as $command) {
20.         $pdo->exec($command);
21.     }
22.     $rm = new Roster($db);
23.     $rm->pdo = $pdo;
24.     $rm->current_season = 19;
25.     $rm->previous_season = 18;
26.     $expected = 'TST McTesterton [UC19]';
27.
28.     // Act
29.     $response = $rm->getById(1);
30.
31.     // Assert
32.     $this->assertEquals($expected, $response['display_name']);
33. }
```

Now this test ... fails?

```
Failed asserting that two strings are equal.
Expected :'TST McTesterton [UC19]'
Actual   :'TST McTesterton'
```

I guess I need to take a look at my assumptions in the code itself about how it is determining whether or not to add the uncarded indicator to the player description. In the code, this appears to be the logic it is using.

IF the uncarded value is the same as previous season OR the uncarded value is the same as the current season THEN add the uncarded indicator to the player's display name

My data seems to match what I want, but I wonder if I should be more strict and make sure to do a proper integer-to-integer comparison because I am using the === operator. Let me make this change to the code we are testing:

```
if ((int)$response['uncarded'] === (int)$this->previous_season
   || (int)$response['uncarded'] === (int)$this->current_season) {
   $response['display_name'] .= ' [UC' . $response['uncarded'] . ']';
}
```

Now, the test passes. This is exactly the situation you will encounter when writing tests after the fact. Your code will often work correctly until you have an edge case come up that has you scratching your head for a moment. With that test passing, it's time to move on to writing a test which makes sure transaction log entries are being generated as expected.

The code for storing the transaction log entries is a function not attached to an object (very old-school thinking by me at the time) and does an insert into our database table. This does not need to be tested at all. If you can't do inserts into the database, you probably have other problems you need to be worrying about.

```
1.  function transaction_log($ibl_team, $log_entry, $db)
2.  {
3.     $insert = $db->newInsert();
4.     $insert->into('transaction_log')
5.        ->cols(
6.           [
7.              'ibl_team' => $ibl_team,
8.              'log_entry' => $log_entry,
9.              'transaction_date' => 'NOW()'
10.          ]
11.       );
```

```
12.     $pdo = new PDO('pgsql:host=localhost;dbname=ibl_stats;user=;password=');
13.     $sth = $pdo->prepare($insert->getStatement());
14.     return $sth->execute($insert->getBindValues());
15. }
```

So, what about some code that handles creating the log entries? I dug around and found an example in the code that processes trades:

```
1.  // Now add entries into the transactions table
2.  $team1_trade_report = implode(', ', $team1_trade_players);
3.  $team2_trade_report = implode(', ', $team2_trade_players);
4.  $team1_transaction="Trades {$team1_trade_report} to {$team1} for {$team2_trade_report}";
5.  $team2_transaction="Trades {$team2_trade_report} to {$team2} for {$team1_trade_report}";
6.
7.  require_once 'transaction_log.php';
8.  transaction_log($team2, $team1_transaction, $db);
9.  transaction_log($team1, $team2_transaction, $db);
```

Okay, so nothing that is using an object that we could test. How are $team1_trade_players and $team2_trade_players being built?

```
1.  foreach ($data1 as $playerInfo) {
2.      list($dataSet, $playerId) = explode('_', $playerInfo);
3.      $playerInfo = $rosterModel->getById($playerId);
4.
5.      if ($playerInfo['ibl_team'] !== $team1) {
6.          $team1_trade_players[] = trim($playerInfo['display_name']);
7.          $rosterModel->updatePlayerTeam($team1, $playerId, $team2TradeComment);
8.          $rosterModel->makeInactive($playerId);
9.      }
10. }
11.
12. foreach ($data2 as $playerInfo) {
13.     list($dataSet, $playerId) = explode('_', $playerInfo);
14.     $playerInfo = $rosterModel->getById($playerId);
15.
16.     if ($playerInfo['ibl_team'] !== $team2) {
17.         $team2_trade_players[] = trim($playerInfo['display_name']);
18.         $rosterModel->updatePlayerTeam($team2, $playerId, $team1TradeComment);
19.         $rosterModel->makeInactive($playerId);
20.     }
21. }
```

This is a point where I am making a judgment call about how much extra work I wish to do. This code is using the getById() method I refactored to make sure it was correctly adding the uncarded indicator to players' info. Do I really need to create a separate object which processes an array of player details and creates the log entry, which is, in turn, handed over to by transaction_log() function? I think I am better served going through any code generating transaction log entries and make sure they are using RosterModel methods that are tested.

Searching some more, I found this code snippet that is being used whenever one or more players are being released from a team.

```php
1. if (isset($_POST['release'])) { $release = true; }
2.
3. if ($release === true) {
4.     $release_list = $_POST['release'];
5.     $released_players = [];
6.
7.     /** @var array $release_list */
8.     foreach ($release_list as $player_id) {
9.         $info = $roster->getById($player_id);
10.        $player_name = trim($info['tig_name']);
11.
12.        if ($roster->isUncarded($player_name)) {
13.            $uc_value = $roster->getUncardedValue($player_name);
14.            $player_name .= " [UC {$uc_value}]";
15.        }
16.
17.        $released_players[] = $player_name;
18.    }
19.
20.    $log_entry = 'Releases ' .implode(', ', $released_players);
21.    transaction_log($ibl_team, $log_entry, $db);
22.    $roster->releasePlayerByList($release_list);
23.    include 'templates/modify_roster/release.php';
24. }
```

I think I can refactor this code to use a different method, and be confident it is doing the correct thing when generating the log entry.

```
1. if ($release === true) {
2.     $release_list = $_POST['release'];
3.     $released_players = [];
4.
5.     /** @var array $release_list */
6.     foreach ($release_list as $player_id) {
7.         $info = $roster->getById($player_id);
8.         $released_players[] = $info['display_name'];
9.     }
10.
11.     $log_entry = 'Releases ' . implode(', ', $released_players);
12.     transaction_log($ibl_team, $log_entry, $db);
13.     $roster->releasePlayerByList($release_list);
14.     include 'templates/modify_roster/release.php';
15. }
```

So now I have code doing the exact same thing it was before but with fewer lines of code. In addition, it is using code I have written a test for to confirm an edge case (Is this player uncarded?) is being correctly handled.

As you get deeper into writing tests for an existing application, you will find this approach to be very useful:

- What behavior am I testing for?
- What does the code that handles this behavior look like?
- What would a test for the behavior look like?
- What dependencies do we have?
- Do those dependencies need to change or can we use the real thing?
- Do we need to challenge assumptions about how the code actually works?
- Do we need to change the code to make our test pass?
- Do we have a test that passes?

In the examples above, you can see I followed every one of those steps. I have often told folks that testing is all about focusing on small bits of work and iterating on them until a single question is answered: Does this specific code display this specific behavior that I am expecting? So much of the work is just following a list like the one I have shared above and answering that high-level question at the end of it.

Sometimes circumstances dictate that you are writing tests after you have a working application. This doesn't mean you can't start writing tests. Just be prepared to make choices about your desired outcomes. You will likely have to change some code to make things testable. You will discover that some things don't work the way you thought they did.

In the end, what you are looking for is a series of tests that give you confidence that if you change something, you have some tests that might be able to tell you that you've broken something. Like transaction log entries. Again.

Chapter

8

Refactoring Helpers

Tests are code you write to make sure other code behaves as expected. They need the same type of care and attention that you should be giving the code they're testing. A lot of the same ways we approach refactoring application code applies to our testing code. In this chapter, I want to show you how I took an existing test helper and refactored it to be more useful.

8. Refactoring Helpers

First, I need to give you some context. The OSS project I have done the most work on is OpenCFP; a self-hosted PHP application conference organizers can use to collect and rate conference talk proposals. It has a lot of tests. Not as many as I want it to, but I am just one person with a finite amount of time to spend on things. So are my contributors.

So I feel the need to be both pragmatic and disciplined at the same time, if that makes sense. We marked a helper method for future removal by adding an annotation to the DocBlock for that method. Here's the one I'm going to refactor:

```
1. /**
2.  * @deprecated
3.  *
4.  * @param array $properties
5.  *
6.  * @return Model\User|\PHPUnit_Framework_MockObject_MockObject
7.  */
8. private function createUserMock(array $properties = []): Model\User
9. {
10.     $user = $this->createMock(Model\User::class);
11.
12.     $user
13.         ->expects($this->any())
14.         ->method('__get')
15.         ->willReturnCallback(function (string $property) use ($properties) {
16.             if (\array_key_exists($property, $properties)) {
17.                 return $properties[$property];
18.             }
19.         });
20.
21.     return $user;
22. }
```

By the end of the refactor, this helper should be doing the same thing: Create a dependency that can be used by the existing tests. So, where do we start?

The test suite for OpenCFP uses both Mockery and Prophecy, two libraries for creating test doubles. If I had really strong feelings, I would probably choose one of these tools and then mark helper methods using the library I did not choose as deprecated, or add comments in the tests to indicate it needs to be modified.

I don't think there is one that is "right" for the project. I started off using Mockery and then tried out some tests using Prophecy, and I really can't make up my mind! I do need something to help me make that decision, though.

Looking at the test class I am refactoring parts of, it seems like the reason it has been marked as deprecated is because we created a test double that is substituting the output of a PHP magic method call (in this case __get()) with an expected value.

This is considered a bad testing practice–here is a quote from the documentation for Mockery about it:

> *PHP magic methods which are prefixed with a double underscore, e.g. __set(), pose a particular problem in mocking and unit testing in general. It is strongly recommended that unit tests and mock objects do not directly refer to magic methods. Instead, refer only to the virtual methods and properties these magic methods simulate.*

Okay, if I'm not going to create a double using either Mockery or Prophecy, what should I do? As always, let's think about what it is we need here. We need something that can act as a user object and contains expected values for properties we are passing into it. I think we could create a fake using an anonymous class.

As a sanity check, let's make sure all the tests pass before I start refactoring that method. I am doing this work with PhpStorm, JetBrains' excellent IDE for PHP users. I configured it to use what the project is using for PHPUnit–PHPUnit installed via Composer.

```
/usr/local/bin/php -dxdebug.remote_mode=jit \
 /Users/chartjes/Sites/opencfp/vendor/phpunit/phpunit/phpunit \
 --no-configuration OpenCFP\Test\Unit\Domain\Speaker\SpeakerProfileTest \
 /Users/chartjes/Sites/opencfp/tests/Unit/Domain/Speaker/SpeakerProfileTest.php \
 --teamcity
PHPUnit 7.5.8 by Sebastian Bergmann and contributors.


Time: 307 ms, Memory: 10.00 MB

OK (45 tests, 45 assertions)

Process finished with exit code 0
```

Everything passes. Here's what the helper looks like now:

```
1.  /**
2.   * @param array $properties
3.   * @return Model\User
4.   */
5.  private function createUserMock(array $properties = []): Model\User
6.  {
7.      $user = new class extends Model\User {
8.          public $properties;
9.
10.         public function __get($property)
11.         {
12.             if (\array_key_exists($property, $this->properties)) {
13.                 return $this->properties[$property];
14.             }
15.         }
16.
17.         public function __set($property, $value)
18.         {
19.             $this->properties[$property] = $value;
20.             return;
21.         }
22.     };
23.     $user->properties = $properties;
24.
25.     return $user;
26. }
```

Re-run the tests and make sure this refactor did not break anything.

```
/usr/local/bin/php -dxdebug.remote_mode=jit \
 /Users/chartjes/Sites/opencfp/vendor/phpunit/phpunit/phpunit \
 --no-configuration OpenCFP\Test\Unit\Domain\Speaker\SpeakerProfileTest \
 /Users/chartjes/Sites/opencfp/tests/Unit/Domain/Speaker/SpeakerProfileTest.php \
 --teamcity
PHPUnit 7.5.8 by Sebastian Bergmann and contributors.

Time: 301 ms, Memory: 10.00 MB

OK (45 tests, 45 assertions)

Process finished with exit code 0
```

Excellent! The test suite still passes, and I have fixed the deprecated method.

Chapter

9

Testing APIs

Most of the work I have done surrounding testing has focused on testing application code. This works quite well for helping design testable code and for preventing future regressions. But there are many more things that need to get tested beyond application code.

The work I have been doing at Mozilla consists of writing tests for services that are used internally. Often, that takes the form of a test suite that is run whenever a deployment of the service happens to our staging and production environments. Although this work has been done in Python, the approach is 100% transferable to PHP.

There are two approaches you can take in testing APIs. Both involve using a different set of tools, but the outcome is the same: Do I have confidence that my API continues to work as expected?

As in other chapters, all the test output is captured from inside JetBrains' PHP IDE PhpStorm.

Response Validation

The first method I want to talk about is one where you make calls to the API and examine the response to make sure the responses you get back are what you expect. For this example, I am going to be using a publicly-available API. One of my hobbies is playing the collectible card game Magic: The Gathering. Whenever I am looking for information on a card, I go to the website Scryfall[1] to do searches. The site is powered by an API, which they have done a very good job of documenting over at https://scryfall.com/docs/api/.

I want to write a test to verify that if I make an API call that is supposed to give me a list of details about Magic cards, I get back a response containing things I am expecting to see. Now, I am not 100% sure that list API request that I am guaranteed to get the same response. So, instead of looking for specific values, I will write a test to verify the fields we are expecting to see do exist.

As always, I start with a failing test.

```php
1. <?php
2. declare(strict_types=1);
3.
4. class ApiResponseTest extends PHPUnit\Framework\TestCase
5. {
6.     /**
7.      * @test
8.      */
9.     public function it_finds_a_page_of_cards(): void
10.     {
11.         $this->assertTrue(false);
12.     }
13. }
```

_____

[1] Scryfall: https://scryfall.com

Next, I'll come up with my Arrange-Act-Assert steps for the test, done as pseudocode.

```
1.  public function it_finds_a_page_of_cards(): void
2.  {
3.      // Arrange
4.      /**
5.       * What are the fields we want to see?
6.       * What is the API call we are making?
7.       */
8.
9.      // Act
10.     /**
11.      * Make the API call
12.      * Turn the JSON response into something we can compare
13.      */
14.
15.     // Assert
16.     /**
17.      * Assert that the response matches our expectation
18.      */
19.     $this->assertTrue(false);
20. }
```

Now, I'll turn that pseudocode into actual code.

```
1.  public function it_finds_a_page_of_cards(): void
2.  {
3.      // Arrange
4.      $expected_fields = ['object', 'total_cards', 'has_more', 'next_page'];
5.      $api_url = 'https://api.scryfall.com/cards?page=1';
6.
7.      // Act
8.      $response = json_decode(
9.          file_get_contents($api_url),
10.         true,
11.         512,
12.         JSON_THROW_ON_ERROR
13.     );
14.
15.     // Assert
16.     foreach ($expected_fields as $field) {
17.         $this->assertArrayHasKey($field, $response);
18.     }
19. }
```

Does the test pass?

```
Testing started at 1:54 p.m. ...
/usr/local/bin/php -dxdebug.remote_mode=jit /usr/local/bin/phpunit \
  --no-configuration --filter "/(::it_finds_a_page_of_cards)( .*)?$/" \
  ApiResponseTest /Users/chartjes/grumpy-guide/test/api_response_test.php \
  --teamcity
PHPUnit 8.3.4 by Sebastian Bergmann and contributors.


Time: 409 ms, Memory: 14.00 MB

OK (1 test, 4 assertions)
```

Next, I want to write a test for when I can get a guarantee that the API request I am going to make will be the same no matter how many times I call it. After looking at their documentation, it appears they are using unique IDs to represent cards in their database. I'll build a test that makes one of these specific calls and then make sure some of the fields in the response contain values I am expecting. Here's what the test looks like:

```
1. public function it_gets_card_details_as_expected(): void
2. {
3.     // Arrange
4.     $card_id = '9ff745f8-8fc2-4f88-ba25-03f8b9ae4932';
5.     $api_url = 'https://api.scryfall.com/cards/' . $card_id;
6.
7.     // Act
8.     $response = json_decode(
9.         file_get_contents($api_url),
10.        true,
11.        512,
12.        JSON_THROW_ON_ERROR
13.    );
14.
15.    // Assert
16.    $this->assertEquals('card', $response['object']);
17.    $this->assertEquals($card_id, $response['id']);
18.    $this->assertEquals('Dusk // Dawn', $response['name']);
19. }
```

My test passes.

```
/usr/local/bin/php -dxdebug.remote_mode=jit /usr/local/bin/phpunit \
 --no-configuration --filter "/(::it_gets_card_details_as_expected)( .*)?$/" \
 ApiResponseTest /Users/chartjes/grumpy-guide/test/api_response_test.php \
 --teamcity
PHPUnit 8.3.4 by Sebastian Bergmann and contributors.


Time: 1.21 seconds, Memory: 12.00 MB

OK (1 test, 3 assertions)
```

These sorts of tests are pretty straightforward, but they might not provide enough value depending on the types of responses we would get back. I could write a much more comprehensive test that checks for the existence of a larger number of fields, but I still have some potential issues. What if the response contains additional fields I'm not expecting? Or what if the value for a field changes from an integer to a string? Most APIs change over time and I want my tests to be able to change with them. For scenarios like this, my best choice is to switch to doing schema validation tests.

API Schema Validation

There is a standard for describing your APIs, called OpenAPI. From the website for the specification:

The OpenAPI Specification (OAS) defines a standard, language-agnostic interface to RESTful APIs which allows both humans and computers to discover and understand the capabilities of the service without access to source code, documentation, or through network traffic inspection. When properly defined, a consumer can understand and interact with the remote service with a minimal amount of implementation logic. An OpenAPI definition can then be used by documentation generation tools to display the API, code generation tools to generate servers and clients in various programming languages, testing tools, and many other use cases. This is of interest to programmers because it allows for a development-with-testing workflow that looks like this:

- API developers build their API
- They document it using tools that support generating an OpenAPI specification
- Tests can be written by validating responses against the specification

The important point to make here is these sorts of tests are not about the actual content of the response. I'm not necessarily concerned with specific values, like IDs or timestamps. What I'm trying to accomplish is to make sure whatever data is in the response conforms to expectations of field names and data types.

From a high level, here is what the tests are trying to accomplish:

- Get the OpenAPI schema for the API you are testing
- Make a request to the API
- Validate that response against your schema

For all the examples below, I am using OpenAPI 3.x as the standard for documenting your API. Swagger is the old way of documenting your API, so I highly encourage folks to move to (or use from the beginning) OpenAPI 3.x. More details on using OpenAPI and some associated tools can be found at OpenAPI.Tools[2] and some excellent advice on building APIs with OpenAPI specifications can be found at https://apisyouwonthate.com. Many thanks to Phil Sturgeon and Matthew Trask for pointing me to some very helpful resources for APIs.

Get the Open API Schema for the API You Are Testing

For these examples, I am going to use a publicly available API with an OpenAPI schema. You can see this API at https://petstore.swagger.io.

The next step is to convert it from Swagger to OpenAPI. OpenAPI.Tools has a list of tools they recommend. Again, pick one that resonates with you. In my case (because I do a lot of work testing things with Python), I went with pyswagger[3]. After downloading the YAML spec for Petstore, I converted it and ended up with a YAML file that is OpenAPI 3.x compliant.

But I wasn't done yet–I installed Speccy[4] and used it to validate this new document, fixing any errors I found. I, then, created a directory in my test directory called specs and copied my new spec file into that directory.

Make a Request to the API

Before I go any further, let me create the skeleton of my first validation test.

---

[2] OpenAPI.Tools: https://openapi.tools
[3] pyswagger: https://github.com/mission-liao/pyswagger
[4] Speccy: https://github.com/wework/speccy

```
/**
 * @test
 */
public function it_validates_getPetById(): void
{
    $this->assertTrue(false);
}
```

Now, I build the request I want to make to the API.

```
1.  public function it_validates_getPetById(): void
2.  {
3.      $uri = 'https://petstore.swagger.io/v2/pet/1';
4.      $responseData = json_decode(
5.          file_get_contents($uri),
6.          true,
7.          512,
8.          JSON_THROW_ON_ERROR
9.      );
10.
11.     // other code below...
12. }
```

For validating those responses, I took some OpenAPI.Tools advice and chose to use OpenAPI-Validator, which you can install using Composer (as a development dependency instead of placing it in production, which is always a good idea).

```
composer req --dev mmal/openapi-validator
```

Now, I want to share something with you. Different OpenAPI validation tools use different techniques for deciding if your spec is valid. Speccy said my spec was OpenAPI compliant once I fixed the problems it reported. When I used OpenAPI-validator, well, it expressed its own ideas on what a valid API is. When I added the code that validates the spec I have, it reported many errors I corrected until everything seemed fine.

As annoying as it was to iterate through the errors, it drives home the point that the job of the specification to tell you whether or not you are doing things correctly. Much like unit tests, a good and thorough specification means you do not waste time debugging errors that are easily caught.

So, following the documentation, I added in the code that validates the specification and then makes sure the response I got back matches our expectations.

```
1.  // Added these dependencies that we needed at the top of the file
2.  use Mmal\OpenapiValidator\Validator;
3.  use Symfony\Component\Yaml\Yaml;
4.
5.  public function it_validates_getPetById(): void
6.  {
7.      $uri = 'https://petstore.swagger.io/v2/pet/1';
8.      $responseData = json_decode(
9.          file_get_contents($uri),
10.         true,
11.         512,
12.         JSON_THROW_ON_ERROR
13.     );
14.     $validator = new Validator(Yaml::parse(
15.         file_get_contents(__DIR__ . '/specs/api.yaml'))
16.     );
17.     $result = $validator->validateBasedOnRequest(
18.         '/pet/{petId}',
19.         'GET',
20.         200,
21.         $responseData
22.     );
23.     $this->assertFalse($result->hasErrors());
24. }
```

Okay, I will explain this whole test from top to bottom.

First, I make my call to the API, getting back a JSON response that I decode and store in $responseData. Next, I use the Validator object in combination with a YAML parser to take a look at my spec file and validate it.

This next step requires some more explanation. When you use the validateBasedOnRequest() method, you need to provide the following things:

- The path as outlined in the OpenAPI spec for the call you are testing
- Which HTTP method you used for the request
- The HTTP status code you are expecting
- The JSON-decoded data you are expecting to see

With that information, we round out the test by making an assertion that we have to errors when comparing the contents of the response to our specification. Does the test pass?

```
/usr/local/bin/php -dxdebug.remote_mode=jit /usr/local/bin/phpunit \
 --no-configuration --filter "/(::it_validates_getPetById)( .*)?$/" \
 ApiResponseTest /Users/chartjes/grumpy-guide/test/api_response_test.php \
 --teamcity
PHPUnit 8.3.4 by Sebastian Bergmann and contributors.


Time: 612 ms, Memory: 12.00 MB

OK (1 test, 1 assertion)
```

How about a test that proves the validation works? I'll create an API response with an incorrect value in it, and the test should then report errors with validation.

```
1.  /**
2.   * @test
3.   */
4.  public function it_catches_invalid_responses(): void
5.  {
6.      // Arrange
7.      $invalidResponse = '
8.          {
9.            "id": "0",
10.           "category": {
11.            "id": 0,
12.            "name": "string"
13.           },
14.           "name": "doggie",
15.           "photoUrls": [
16.            "string"
17.           ],
18.           "tags": [
19.            {
20.              "id": 0,
21.              "name": "string"
22.            }
23.           ],
24.           "status": "available"
25.          }';
26.
27.      $validator = new Validator(Yaml::parse(
28.          file_get_contents(__DIR__ . '/specs/api.yaml'))
29.      );
```

```
30.
31.    // Act
32.    $result = $validator->validateBasedOnRequest(
33.        '/pet/{petId}',
34.        'GET',
35.        200,
36.        json_decode($invalidResponse, true, 512, JSON_THROW_ON_ERROR),
37.    );
38.
39.    // Assert
40.    $this->assertTrue($result->hasErrors());
41. }
```

The test passes.

```
/usr/local/bin/php -dxdebug.remote_mode=jit /usr/local/bin/phpunit \
 --no-configuration --filter "/(::it_catches_invalid_responses)( .*)?$/" \
 ApiResponseTest /Users/chartjes/grumpy-guide/test/api_response_test.php \
 --teamcity
PHPUnit 8.3.4 by Sebastian Bergmann and contributors.


Time: 278 ms, Memory: 12.00 MB

OK (1 test, 1 assertion)

Process finished with exit code 0
```

Validation tests are great for figuring out if your API has changed without anyone realizing it–that uncertainty can lead to bad experiences and weird errors appearing in production. To be perfectly clear, there is extra work involved because someone will have to create and maintain the OpenAPI specifications. You can use tools like Stoplight Studio[5] to create the specification at the same time you are creating your API.

---

[5]   Stoplight Studio: https://stoplight.io

Chapter

10

Data Providers

Why You Should Use Data Providers

One of your main goals should always be writing the bare minimum amount of code in order to solve a particular problem. This is no different when it comes to tests, which are really nothing more than code.

One of the earliest lessons I learned when I started writing comprehensive test suites was to always look for duplication in your tests. Here's an example of a situation where this can happen.

You might be familiar with the FizzBuzz problem[1] problem, if only because it is sometimes presented as a problem to be solved as part of an interview. It is a good problem because it touches on a lot of really elementary basics of programming–you need to understand loops, collections, and conditional statements.

When you write tests for FizzBuzz, what you want to do is pass it a set of values and verify they are FizzBuzzed correctly. This could result in you having multiple tests that are the same, except for the values you are testing with. Data providers give you a way to simplify that process.

A data provider is a way to create multiple sets of testing data which can be passed in as parameters to your test method. You create a method that is available to the class your tests are in that returns an array of values matching the parameters you are passing into your test.

It sounds more complicated than it really is; let's look at an example.

Look at All Those Tests

If you didn't know about data providers, what might your FizzBuzz tests look like?

```php
1. <?php
2. class FizzBuzzTest extends PHPUnit\Framework\TestCase
3. {
4.    public function setup()
5.    {
6.        $this->fb = new FizzBuzz();
7.    }
8.
9.    public function testGetFizz()
10.   {
11.       $expected = 'Fizz';
12.       $input = 3;
13.       $response = $this->fb->check($input);
14.       $this->assertEquals($expected, $response);
15.   }
16.
```

---

[1] FizzBuzz problem: http://en.wikipedia.org/wiki/FizzBuzz

```
17.    public function testGetBuzz()
18.    {
19.        $expected = 'Buzz';
20.        $input = 5;
21.        $response = $this->fb->check($input);
22.        $this->assertEquals($expected, $response);
23.    }
24.
25.    public function testGetFizzBuzz()
26.    {
27.        $expected = 'FizzBuzz';
28.        $input = 15;
29.        $response = $this->fb->check($input);
30.        $this->assertEquals($expected, $response);
31.    }
32.
33.    function testPassThru()
34.    {
35.        $expected = '1';
36.        $input = 1;
37.        $response = $this->fb->check($input);
38.        $this->assertEquals($expected, $response);
39.    }
40. }
```

I'm sure you can see the pattern:

- Multiple input values

- Tests that are extremely similar in setup and execution

- Same assertion being used over and over

Creating Data Providers

A data provider is another method inside your test class that returns an array of results, with each result set being an array itself. Through some magic internal work, PHPUnit converts the returned result set into parameters your test method signature needs to accept.

```
1.    public function fizzBuzzProvider()
2.    {
3.       return [
4.           [1, '1'],
5.           [3, 'Fizz'],
6.           [5, 'Buzz'],
7.           [15, 'FizzBuzz']
8.       ];
9.    }
```

The function name for the provider doesn't matter, but I prefer to give them a readable-as-English name as you might be stumped when a test fails, and PHPUnit tells you about a data provider called 'ex1ch2', or something else equally hard to instantly understand its purpose.

To use the data provider, we have to add an annotation to the DocBlock preceding our test, so PHPUnit knows to use it. Give it the name of the data provider method.

```
1.    /**
2.     * Test for our FizzBuzz object
3.     *
4.     * @dataProvider fizzBuzzProvider
5.     */
6.    public function testFizzBuzz($input, $expected)
7.    {
8.       $response = $this->fb->check($input);
9.       $this->assertEquals($expected, $response);
10.   }
```

Now we have just one test (less code to maintain) and can add scenarios to our heart's content via the data provider (even better). We have also learned the skill of applying some critical analysis to the testing code we are writing to ensure we are only writing the tests we actually need.

When using a data provider, PHPUnit will run the test method each time for every set of data being passed in by the provider. If the test fails, it will indicate which index in the associative array was being used for that test run.

More Complex Examples

Don't feel like you can only have really simple data providers. All you need to do is return an array of arrays, with each result set matching the parameters your testing method is expecting. Here's a more complex example:

```
1.    public function complexProvider()
2.    {
3.        // Read in some data from a CSV file
4.        $fp = fopen("./fixtures/data.csv");
5.        $response = [];
6.
7.        while ($data = fgetcsv($fp, 1000, ",")) {
8.            $response[] = array($data[0], $data[1], $data[2]);
9.        }
10.
11.       fclose($fp);
12.
13.       return $response;
14.   }
```

Don't think you need to limit yourself in what your data providers are allowed to do. The goal is to create useful data sets for testing purposes.

Data Provider Tricks

Since data providers return associative arrays, you can assign them a more descriptive key to help with debugging. For example, I could refactor the data provider for my FizzBuzz test:

```
return [
    'one'   => [1, '1'],
    'fizz'  => [3, 'Fizz'],
    'buzz'  => [5, 'Buzz'],
    'fizzbuzz' => [15, 'FizzBuzz']
];
```

Also, data providers don't have to be methods inside the same class. You can use methods in other classes, you just have to set their visibility to public. You can use namespaces as well. Here are two examples that would go into the DocBlock for any test that wants to use a provider in another class:

- `@dataProvider Foo::dataProvider`

- `@dataProvider Grumpy\Helpers\Foo::dataProvider`

This allows you to create helper classes that are just data providers and cut down on the amount of duplicated code you have in your tests themselves.

Final Thoughts

The role of a data provider is to reduce duplication of code in your tests by providing you with a way to have a test use multiple sets of data for inputs and/or expected results. Just like any code, if you realize you are repeating yourself, I suggest taking a look at the test and determine if a data provider is a good fit.

Chapter

11

Wrappers

One of the more challenging tasks is writing unit tests for code which needs to talk to third-party APIs. Given my goal of never speaking to a real web API, how can I do this? The answer is, of course, to use a wrapper.

Wrappers From Up High

The idea I'm presenting is probably some type of software design pattern, but I can't seem to find my copy of the very famous "Gang of Four" Design Patterns book. Let's just call it a wrapper.

Create an object which accepts as a constructor parameter another object which knows how to speak to the API. This wrapper object often duplicates the methods of the main API object to reduce confusion about functionality. Let me show you an example.

I took to Twitter and asked for some examples of free-to-use, publicly-accessible web APIs that generate some useful information. I got numerous suggestions, but the one I went with was JSONPlaceholder[1]. It describes itself as a "free online REST service that you can use whenever you need some fake data." It sounds like just the thing I need.

Of course, I'll start with a test:

```php
1. <?php
2. declare(strict_types=1);
3.
4. require '../vendor/autoload.php';
5. require '../src/JsonPlaceHolder.php';
6.
7. class JsonPlaceHolderTest extends PHPUnit\Framework\TestCase
8. {
9.     /**
10.      * @test
11.      */
12.     public function callToPostsReturns100Posts()
13.     {
14.         $jph = new JsonPlaceHolder();
15.         $posts = $jph->getPosts();
16.         $this->assertCount(100, $posts);
17.     }
18. }
```

It fails because I haven't written any code yet.

What should my JSONPlaceholder object look like to pass the test?

---

[1]   JSONPlaceholder: http://jsonplaceholder.typicode.com

```
1. <?php
2. declare(strict_types=1);
3.
4. class JsonPlaceHolder
5. {
6.     public $url = 'http://jsonplaceholder.typicode.com';
7.
8.     public function getPosts()
9.     {
10.         $response = file_get_contents("{$this->url}/posts");
11.         return json_decode($response, true, 512, JSON_THROW_ON_ERROR);
12.     }
13. }
```

The test now passes.

```
usr/local/bin/php -dxdebug.remote_mode=jit /usr/local/bin/phpunit \
 --no-configuration JsonPlaceHolderTest \
 /Users/chartjes/grumpy-guide/test/JsonPlaceHolderTest.php --teamcity \
 --cache-result-file=/Users/chartjes/grumpy-guide/.phpunit.result.cache
PHPUnit 8.3.4 by Sebastian Bergmann and contributors.


Time: 292 ms, Memory: 12.00 MB

OK (1 test, 1 assertion)

Process finished with exit code 0
```

What do I do if I want to write some unit tests for this code? I don't want to actually talk to the web API, so we can create a wrapper. I'll create a simple pass-through wrapper.

```
1. <?php
2. declare(strict_types=1);
3.
4. class JsonPlaceHolderWrapper
5. {
6.     public $jph;
7.
8.     public function __construct(JsonPlaceHolder $jph)
9.     {
10.         $this->jph = $jph;
11.     }
12.
```

```
13.    public function getPosts(): array
14.    {
15.        return $this->jph->getPosts();
16.    }
17. }
```

Then, I update my test so it uses the wrapper:

```
1.  <?php
2.  declare(strict_types=1);
3.
4.  require '../vendor/autoload.php';
5.  require '../src/JsonPlaceHolder.php';
6.  require '../src/JsonPlaceHolderWrapper.php';
7.
8.  class JsonPlaceHolderTest extends PHPUnit\Framework\TestCase
9.  {
10.     /**
11.      * @test
12.      */
13.     public function callToPostsReturns100Posts()
14.     {
15.         $jph = new JsonPlaceHolder();
16.         $wrapper = new JsonPlaceHolderWrapper($jph);
17.         $posts = $wrapper->getPosts();
18.         $this->assertCount(100, $posts);
19.     }
20. }
```

The test passes.

```
/usr/local/bin/php -dxdebug.remote_mode=jit /usr/local/bin/phpunit \
 --no-configuration --filter "/(::callToPostsReturns100Posts)( .*)?$/" \
 JsonPlaceHolderTest /Users/chartjes/grumpy-guide/test/JsonPlaceHolderTest.php \
 --teamcity --cache-result-file=/Users/chartjes/grumpy-guide/.phpunit.result.cache
PHPUnit 8.3.4 by Sebastian Bergmann and contributors.


Time: 339 ms, Memory: 12.00 MB

OK (1 test, 1 assertion)

Process finished with exit code 0
```

Now that I'm using the wrapper, I can create something which behaves like the JSONPlaceholder object I'm expecting but doesn't speak to the API at all.

```php
1.  <?php
2.  declare(strict_types=1);
3.
4.  require '../src/JsonPlaceHolder.php';
5.
6.  class FakeJsonPlaceHolder extends JsonPlaceHolder
7.  {
8.      public function getPosts()
9.      {
10.         /**
11.          * We know that a record should look something like this:
12.          * {
13.         "userId": 1,
14.         "id": 1,
15.         "title": "sunt aut facere repellat provident occaecati",
16.         "body": "quia et suscipit suscipit recusandae consequuntur"
17.         }
18.          */
19.         $response = [];
20.         $x = 1;
21.         while ($x <= 100) {
22.             $post = [
23.                 'userId' => 1,
24.                 'id' => uniqid('', true),
25.                 'title' => uniqid('', true),
26.                 'body' => uniqid('', true)
27.             ];
28.             $response[] = $post;
29.             $x++;
30.         }
31.
32.         return $response;
33.     }
34. }
```

Next, I change the test to use the fake object.

```
1.  <?php
2.  declare(strict_types=1);
3.
4.  require '../vendor/autoload.php';
5.  require 'FakeJsonPlaceHolder.php';
6.  require '../src/JsonPlaceHolderWrapper.php';
7.
8.  class JsonPlaceHolderTest extends PHPUnit\Framework\TestCase
9.  {
10.     /**
11.      * @test
12.      */
13.     public function callToPostsReturns100Posts()
14.     {
15.         $jph = new FakeJsonPlaceHolder();
16.         $wrapper = new JsonPlaceHolderWrapper($jph);
17.         $posts = $wrapper->getPosts();
18.         $this->assertCount(100, $posts);
19.     }
20. }
```

The test still passes:

```
/usr/local/bin/php -dxdebug.remote_mode=jit /usr/local/bin/phpunit \
 --no-configuration --filter "/(::callToPostsReturns100Posts)( .*)?$/" \
 JsonPlaceHolderTest /Users/chartjes/grumpy-guide/test/JsonPlaceHolderTest.php \
 --teamcity --cache-result-file=/Users/chartjes/grumpy-guide/.phpunit.result.cache
PHPUnit 8.3.4 by Sebastian Bergmann and contributors.


Time: 163 ms, Memory: 12.00 MB

OK (1 test, 1 assertion)

Process finished with exit code 0
```

The downside to this approach is you are exposing some of the implementation details of your dependencies via your tests. This is a very simple example of creating a test double, but I have written tests which required several layers of doubles returning doubles return doubles. It's fragile, and the tests easily no longer represent reality if the dependency itself has changed.

Chapter

12

Metatesting

If you're not familiar with Magic: The Gathering, I can only describe it as chess, but with new pieces constantly being made. Older pieces can be sold on a secondary market for a lot of money. You acquire cards, either through purchasing or trading with others, and build decks out of the cards to play the game. It's the world's most popular collectible card game with a dizzying array of cards and formats to choose from.

One of the interesting concepts to come out of competitive tournament play is the idea of the metagame. It's the label which has been attached to the decks people choose and the strategies they are likely to use. High-level players (yes, there are even professional players) gain advantages by understanding the metagame for a tournament they are going to play in and trying to figure out what decks and strategies are most likely to give them an edge.

What does this have to do with writing tests for your PHP code? We can take this concept of the metagame and apply it to testing practices. Clearly, there are some practices which are good, and some which are not-so-good. I want to examine some of these to help you find things that might lead to better outcomes for your application. Remember, what you are really trying to do with tests is to prevent regressions and make sure the application is useful to the people who are going to use it. Nothing else matters in the end.

So what does the testing "metagame" look like from my perspective?

Mature Testing Tools Are Available

PHP developers are spoiled for choice when it comes to testing tools. The gold standard for unit testing tools, PHPUnit (a testing tool that promotes the use of the xUnit testing pattern), is stable and mature. I don't want to be "back in my day you had to do things both ways, uphill, in the snow," but as I am writing this at the end of 2019, there is a great ecosystem surrounding PHPUnit and lots of tools that are both complementary and use PHPUnit as a base to build on.

When you consider tools such as Behat (which is a testing tool that promotes the use of Behavioural-Driven Development for defining tests) or Codeception (a testing tool focused on using browser automation), it is clear there isn't any real excuse for not adopting automated testing practices.

While there is a tendency for developers to reinvent tools rather than modify existing ones, I think we've reached a point where there are some solid testing strategies which have been accepted by the PHP community. Pick a tool and get started.

You can either write tests you can automate, or you can write tests that you can manually perform. Either way, you are writing tests. Why not get the computer, which has no biases about what parts of the application are important, to run the tests for you?

Yes, there was a time when these tools were not easy to install, and there was not a lot of information available on how to use them in a comprehensive way. But not anymore.

Test your code. It will save you time and money and allow you to focus on solving problems instead of fixing bugs that could've been prevented from making it into production.

Open Source Drives Acceptance

It is highly unlikely any open source code you rely on to get your day-to-day work done has no tests. Every popular web application framework for PHP has a comprehensive test suite along with instructions on how to run it. The database you use has comprehensive tests. The web server your application relies on has comprehensive tests.

Personally, I avoid using third-party libraries which don't have a test suite of their own. In my mind, it speaks volumes about the author(s) commitment to quality and longevity in their code.

In fact, many projects won't accept bug fixes without a test proving the fix works as expected. For people looking to get into contributing code to OSS projects, you'll get a crash course in how tests are written by simply looking at the ones which already exist.

Proof Exists to Back the Promises

In 2008, a paper was published about the impact of TDD, which looked at case studies conducted by Microsoft and IBM. You can find the study online[1].

Several teams were given the same problem to solve via code. Some of those teams were asked to use TDD, others were not. The results of this study were very interesting and are actual evidence of the value writing tests for your code.

I encourage you to read the actual paper (it's only 14 pages), but the big takeaway is this: The projects using TDD had 40-90% fewer reported defects than ones who didn't use it, but they took 15-35% longer to get the job done.

If you are into using statistics to your advantage in discussions with people, it can be summarized as "for an extra day a week we can have up to 90% fewer bugs making it into production." It's a very powerful argument to make.

Testing Moves Bug Fixing to a Cheaper Part of the Cycle

This particular concept was one which took me a few years to fully understand. Much like the argument about the benefit of TDD being fewer production bugs existing with a small increase in development time, the "shifting the cost" argument is a very powerful one.

The cheapest time (in terms of developer time and resources committed) to find a bug in your code is during initial development and exploratory testing by the developer. If you practice TDD, you're writing tests for how you expect the code to work and then writing code until those tests pass. Let's call this cost X.

---

[1]   online: http://research.microsoft.com/en-us/groups/ese/nagappan_tdd.pdf

Once the developer is "done," the code then needs to move from a state of "development" to a state of "quality assurance." This can take many forms, such as code review, a staging environment where the code changes are tested. The cost of finding a bug during code review could be anywhere from 2X to 10X.

Why? Think about it–you now have to go back and verify not only the bug but ensure the code changes you have made won't result in something else breaking. Then, you have to move the code back out of "development" and into "quality assurance" again. Don't ever kid yourself; this process takes time and is often at the mercy of someone else's schedule!

Once you're convinced your code is behaving as expected, it needs to be moved into a state of "deployed." I can tell you from personal experience, the most expensive time to fix a bug is when it has been discovered by a third-party out in the wild. I think a conservative estimate is labeling this as 100X. In fact, let's break this down even further.

First, we have the emotional or "cultural" cost of the bug. Serious production bugs are often accompanied by an environment of panic, and many people chaotically trying to solve the same problem. I have worked for many companies which forced development teams to all stick around to solve a problem–even if you didn't have anything to do with the problem and couldn't help.

If you get enough bugs reaching production, you could end up with deployments becoming super stressful. What happens then? Deployments move to being done outside of "normal" business hours–meaning you end up working either way later or way earlier than normal. "Everyone needs to be here in case there is a problem." In other words, panicking over pushes to production becomes the "new normal" instead of being a non-issue as they should.

The second cost of a production bug is the cost of lost opportunity. If you're in charge of a team working on a project, you must instinctively understand every minute spent fixing a bug found in a released product is a minute not being spent advancing the project's goals. The bug is preventing your team from refactoring old problems or implementing new features. This is a real cost and is very rarely considered.

Well-Documented Build Systems Encourage Continuous Deployment

One of the reasons for committing so many resources towards automated tests is to create automated build systems which take the code that's been written, run all the tests, and if they all pass automatically deploy the code (along with anything else required to support it).

When I first started figuring out how to make this happen, the tool of choice was Jenkins[2]. It's a Java-based automation tool which is ridiculously flexible in how it can help you and has a high number of plugins available. Chances are, if there is something you want to do with Jenkins, someone has figured out how to do it with a plugin.

The idea of build automation is to take things you normally do by hand as part of your deployment and testing process and automate those steps. After all, computers are great at doing what you've told them to do over and over again without complaining! Like with many things, once you've automated how your tests are run, you don't have to think about it anymore. You can save your brainpower for things like making jokes in your company chat or trolling people on social media.

Your options, however, are not limited to just Jenkins. A great alternative for those who don't want to host their own CI server is to use services like Travis CI[3], CircleCI[4], or GitHub Actions[5]. These services allow you to replicate the process you go through when someone grabs your code and wants to run your tests. They all have their own particular syntax and quirks, but they all end up at the same place–a Git-centric system that can react to pull requests or merges and execute a series of steps that should end with your tests being run.

For OpenCFP[6], I have started using GitHub Actions as my build automation tool. When I look at the configuration file for it, it does all the following things for me:

- Checkout the code
- Install the exact versions of PHP I want my tests to be run against
- Install all my dependencies using Composer
- Run a code linter and style fixer against the code
- Run my database migrations
- Build my CSS and JS assets
- Verify all the mappings and schemas for code that uses an ORM
- Run the tests

---

[2] Jenkins: *https://jenkins-ci.org*
[3] Travis CI: *https://travis-ci.org*
[4] CircleCI: *https://circleci.com*
[5] GitHub Actions: *https://github.com/features/actions*
[6] OpenCFP: *https://github.com/opencfp/opencfp*

These are all things I started out doing manually, but I want them automated. In an idealized environment, I would want to do this sort of thing locally. The project does use Composer's "scripts" section to define some tasks I use to do those exact steps above. Again, I want the computer to repeat these tasks for me, over and over again. The likelihood of me making a mistake with one of these steps is a lot higher than if the computer does it.

There Are Awesome Complementary Tools

It's not enough to have tests for your code. It does take a significant amount of discipline to continue writing those tests and staying focused on using Test-Driven Development effectively. Luckily other people have been tackling those same problems and have some solutions I can endorse.

XDebug

First, there is XDebug[7]. XDebug is a PHP extension which allows you to do two things that are useful for PHP developers. The first is that you can use it as a step-through debugger when you are refactoring existing code or just trying to figure out "Why is this code not behaving the way I expect it to?" There are many articles out there on how to install XDebug and configure it to work with your preferred editor or IDE. For many years, I resisted using a debugger, instead relying on tests and printing out debugging statements in my code. It takes a long time to learn new habits, but with some help from PhpStorm, I have been working hard to remember I have a step-through debugger that can show me the contents of variables at my breakpoint. Learning to use a debugger is a skill more programmers of all languages could stand to get better at.

The second thing XDebug is great at for PHP folks is how, in combination with PHPUnit, it can be used to generate code coverage reports. Code coverage is a metric many use to track how much of your code is being executed by your tests. Code bases with very high code coverage percentages (90% and over) tend to be reliable and bug-free. It is possible to get to 100% code coverage, but it's hard to do if you don't build your project using TDD.

To generate your code coverage report, you add some options to the command you are using to run your tests from the CLI, and a report will be generated for you. The most common option is to generate an HTML-based report you can load in your browser to verify what is and isn't covered by your tests.

For OpenCFP, we generate a text-based coverage report. Here's a sample of what it looks like:

---

[7]   XDebug: https://xdebug.org

```
Code Coverage Report:
  2019-12-27 19:36:57

 Summary:
  Classes: 43.69% (45/103)
  Methods: 52.15% (206/395)
  Lines:   42.50% (1085/2553)

\OpenCFP::OpenCFP\Environment
  Methods: 100.00% (12/12)   Lines: 100.00% ( 22/ 22)
\OpenCFP::OpenCFP\Path
  Methods:  75.00% ( 3/ 4)   Lines:  80.00% (  4/  5)
\OpenCFP::OpenCFP\WebPath
  Methods:  66.67% ( 2/ 3)   Lines:  66.67% (  2/  3)
\OpenCFP\Application::OpenCFP\Application\Speakers
  Methods: 100.00% ( 4/ 4)   Lines: 100.00% ( 13/ 13)
\OpenCFP\Http\Action\Profile::OpenCFP\Http\Action\Profile\EditAction
  Methods:  50.00% ( 1/ 2)   Lines:  35.48% ( 11/ 31)
\OpenCFP\Http\Action\Profile::OpenCFP\Http\Action\Profile\ProcessAction
  Methods:  25.00% ( 1/ 4)   Lines:  19.35% ( 12/ 62)
```

(Looks like I've got some work to do improving coverage via testing.)

There are other formats for the code coverage report–it can generate XML-based ones for importing by other tools, or a series of HTML pages you can browse through if you are looking to find specific sections of code that have not been tested.

Like I said before, code coverage is just a number; you can still have bugs and unexpected behavior in a codebase with 100% coverage. 100% coverage, when combined with defensive programming techniques like data validation, filtering inputs, and escaping outputs can really reduce the likelihood of your code having bugs and/or unexpected behavior.

Static Analysis Tools

Tests cannot tell you if you are not using features of the PHP language itself correctly, or even creating very subtle bugs. As PHP moves further down the road of using explicit typing for parameters, return types, and class attributes, a tool that can find instances of type-related bugs is very helpful. In OpenCFP, I have used two tools–PHPStan and Psalm.

PHPStan[8] describes itself as:

---

[8] PHPStan: *https://github.com/phpstan/phpstan*

> *PHPStan focuses on finding errors in your code without actually running it. It catches whole classes of bugs even before you write tests for the code. It moves PHP closer to compiled languages in the sense that the correctness of each line of the code can be checked before you run the actual line.*

OpenCFP has used PHPStan in the past and already has a configuration file and tooling in place to run it. Here's a sample of what PHPStan tells me when I run it against my codebase:

```
------ ---------------------------------------------------------------------
------------------------------------
  Line   src/Http/Action/Talk/UpdateAction.php
------ ---------------------------------------------------------------------
------------------------------------
  74       Property OpenCFP\Http\Action\Talk\UpdateAction::$twig has unknown class OpenCFP\
Http\Action\Talk\Twig\Environment as
           its type.
------ ---------------------------------------------------------------------
------------------------------------


------ ---------------------------------------------------------------------
  Line   src/Infrastructure/Event/TwigGlobalsListener.php
------ ---------------------------------------------------------------------
  45       Property OpenCFP\Infrastructure\Event\TwigGlobalsListener::$twig has unknown class
           OpenCFP\Infrastructure\Event\Twig\Environment as its type.
------ ---------------------------------------------------------------------


------ -------------------------------------------------------------------
  Line   tests/Unit/Domain/Services/ResetEmailerTest.php
------ -------------------------------------------------------------------
  44       Class OpenCFP\Test\Unit\Domain\Services\Twig\Template not found.
------ -------------------------------------------------------------------
```

It seems like I need to take a look at some of my code that is using Twig.

Psalm[9] declares itself as:

> *Psalm is a static analysis tool that attempts to dig into your program and find as many type-related bugs as possible.*

After following the directions for installing and configuring it, here is a sample of what it reports for OpenCFP's codebase:

---

[9] Psalm. *https://psalm.dev*

```
INFO: MissingClosureParamType - src/Infrastructure/Templating/TwigExtension.php:65:50 - Parameter
$route has no provided type
            new TwigFunction('active', function ($route) {


ERROR: PossiblyNullReference - src/Infrastructure/Templating/TwigExtension.php:67:67 - Cannot call
method getRequestUri on possibly null value
                === $this->requestStack->getCurrentRequest()->getRequestUri();


INFO: MissingReturnType - src/Infrastructure/Validation/RequestValidator.php:38:21 - Method
OpenCFP\Infrastructure\Validation\RequestValidator::validate does not have a return type,
expecting void
    public function validate(Request $request, array $rules)


INFO: MissingReturnType - src/Kernel.php:69:21 - Method OpenCFP\Kernel::registerContainerConfigura
tion does not have a return type, expecting void
    public function registerContainerConfiguration(LoaderInterface $loader)


(Other details snipped)

------------------------------
138 errors found
------------------------------
133 other issues found.
You can hide them with --show-info=false
------------------------------
Psalm can automatically fix 14issues.
Run Psalm again with
--alter --issues=MismatchingDocblockReturnType,InvalidReturnType,InvalidFalsableReturnType,Missing
ParamType --dry-run
to see what it can fix.
------------------------------
```

You should be using one of these two tools, which one to choose is really all about personal preference. Either one of them will help you.

One of the reasons I currently prefer Psalm to PHPStan is because it can attempt to fix things that it finds. As I have said many, many times — I prefer to use tools that automate fixing things I might forget to do so I can use my mental energy to solve more difficult problems.

Mutation Testing

The final complementary testing tool I encourage you to take a look at is Infection, a mutation testing tool. From the website for Infection[10]:

> Mutation testing involves modifying a program in small ways. Each mutated version is called a Mutant. To assess the quality of a given test set, these mutants are executed against the input test set to see if the seeded faults can be detected. If the mutated program produces failing tests, this is called a killed mutant. If tests are green with mutated code, then we have an escaped mutant.

If you've ever wondered if there's a tool that can test your tests, then you will find something like Infection valuable. OpenCFP is also configured to use Infection as a development dependency. After following the instructions to install and configure Infection, here is the report it gave me for the codebase:

```
Running initial test suite...

PHPUnit version: 7.5.17

  575 [============================] 8 mins

Generate mutants...

Processing source code files: 119/119
Creating mutated files and processes: 1000/1000
.: killed, M: escaped, S: uncovered, E: fatal error, T: timed out

.MS...S.SSM..M....MM.MM.MM.M..MMMMMMMM.MMM........  (  50 / 1000)
M......M......M......M........S..M...............  ( 100 / 1000)
...M..MS....MSSSSSSSSSSS.............M.M..MMM.MMM.  ( 150 / 1000)
M.M......M.M..M.....M.M..M...........M...........  ( 200 / 1000)
....SSSSM..MM..M.SSSSSMMM.M..SSSSSMMMM.S..MSM.....  ( 250 / 1000)
.MMMM.....M......MM.M.....SSS.SSSSSSSSSSSSSSSSM....  ( 300 / 1000)
..MMMM....MMMMMM.MMMMMMMMMM..MMMMSM.M.SM.M.MMM...M  ( 350 / 1000)
..MM...MMSS.MMMM.......MMMMMM.MMMMMMMMMMM....MS.M..  ( 400 / 1000)
.M............MM.M.MMMSS.....M...................  ( 450 / 1000)
......MMMMMMMMMMMSSMMMMMMMMMMMMMMMMMMMSSSS........  ( 500 / 1000)
....MMMMMMMMMMMMMMM.M....MMM....MM.MSMMMM.M.SM...M  ( 550 / 1000)
...M........M....MM.M......................M...  ( 600 / 1000)
```

---

[10] Infection: https://infection.github.io/guide/

```
........M.MM....SSSS..M.MM...SS.SS....M.SS.......S   ( 650 / 1000)
SS..............................SSSSSSSSSS          ( 700 / 1000)
SSSSSSS........S....MM....SS...............S..S..S   ( 750 / 1000)
.M.....MMM....MMM...........S.S.S.S...SSSS..S.S.    ( 800 / 1000)
.......................S..M..MMSS.MMSSSSSSSSSSS      ( 850 / 1000)
.......................................M..M...MM    ( 900 / 1000)
.........M...........M.............S.M........M..    ( 950 / 1000)
M..M..M......SSSSSSS.........M.........M.......S.M   (1000 / 1000)

1000 mutations were generated:
      629 mutants were killed
      136 mutants were not covered by tests
      235 covered mutants were not detected
        0 errors were encountered
        0 time outs were encountered

Metrics:
        Mutation Score Indicator (MSI): 63%
        Mutation Code Coverage: 86%
        Covered Code MSI: 73%

Please note that some mutants will inevitably be harmless (i.e., false positives).
```

As a rough guide (again, this is just my opinion), the spread between the MSI and the Mutation Code Coverage value is an indication that my tests themselves need some work. The Infection website has more documentation on how to interpret these values and what to do about it.

Chapter

13

Building a Testing Culture

It takes a lot of work to put together the type of environment where testing is an integral part of your daily work. It can't be an afterthought or something that is forgotten when the deadlines get tight. Testing has to become a primary practice, or it will just not work. Let's also make sure we are getting all our terms straight–what does it mean when I start talking about "building a testing culture?"

Primary Goal

The primary goal should be "our developers write tests for any code that goes into production." Anything less than that is an opportunity for those folks with a little less discipline or more anxiety about delivery times to backslide and abandon the primary goal of having tests for all your code.

Primary goals are supposed to be lofty and ambitious–but in this case, they are totally achievable. You absolutely can provide your developers with all the training and support they need to learn how to write tests. You just have to change your behavior and probably challenge a lot of beliefs about programming that you have.

With your primary goal set, let's talk about the secondary goals you need to make the primary goal work.

Tests as First Class Components

Of course, you can't really have a culture that includes testing if you don't have any tests! This is usually the biggest obstacle for any organization to becoming test-centric. Think back to when you were learning to program in PHP–were you taught to write tests? If you were, consider yourself extremely lucky!

It may seem obvious, but the first thing you'll have to do is commit to writing tests for any new code that is written. Yes, this is likely to be painful as your organization makes the transition. Yes, you will probably complain about this. I have been in more than one meeting where people complained their work would've been done if "it wasn't for all these stupid tests I have to write."

Developers, who mostly pride themselves on logic and problem-solving skills, are just as resistant to change as anyone else. It will be hard to get into the habit of always having tests with your code.

If you're looking for a way to ease into adding tests, here are some strategies you can apply.

Tests for Bugs

Any time someone reports a bug, write a test verifying the bug exists. By this, I mean the test should fail; you should know what the correct outcome should be, and then the test generates its own outcome you compare to the expectation.

With a failing test that also has what the correct outcome is supposed to be, you change the code you're testing until the test passes. Now, you have a passing test!

A test suite consisting of fixes for bugs can also show you some common patterns in your code–especially if you feel like you're repeatedly fixing the same type of bugs.

From a mentoring perspective, asking developers new to a project to write test cases that verify bugs exist can be a good strategy. It allows them a chance to explore the codebase and see how things fit together. For some codebases, this will definitely be intimidating. Giving them a chance to learn the codebase through tests is probably less risky than assigning work that needs to go up into production.

Tests for New Features

Any time you add new code, it must come with tests that prove the new code works as expected. This is similar to writing tests for bugs, but in this case, you are using the tests to help you create working code.

In this context of "tests are for new features," Test-Driven Development can really shine. TDD is really a strategy for writing code in a specific way–one which results in code that is testable with low amounts of friction or developer pain.

But it doesn't come without costs. Often, a legacy application is not well-suited to allowing you to write easily tested code. This is a barrier many developers get slammed up against and, as a result, abandon the goal of having tests.

I don't have any shortcuts to make this easier. The pain you feel is neither good, nor bad– it is simply a result of the current architecture of your application. Well-tested apps tend to consist of small modules of code that:

- Accept a small number of inputs
- Does not alter anything other than what was given to it (no side-effects)
- Returns a small number of outputs

When you have code like this, it's easy to test! Most code does not look like that. You will need to rewrite some code; you will need to start to use new strategies; you will end up taking longer than you thought to create new code and the tests that come with it.

The upside to all this is you have tests that act as proof the new feature will work as expected, given the information you have at the time you wrote the code. Good defensive coding habits can help a little, but the truth is that code with unit tests with 100% coverage doesn't always mean your application will work correctly. You still have to connect them together and use them in a way that makes sense. Testing is definitely not a substitute for common sense.

Tests for Refactoring

You might think this is covered by the section on tests for new features, but I feel like they are two different things.

Your definition of refactoring might be different from mine. To me, refactoring is the process of taking code that is working as expected and modifying it to take advantage of new knowledge, techniques, or libraries. The output or final result of the code should not change! If that happens, you're rewriting the code to do something different.

So when it comes to refactoring, this seems to me to be a perfect candidate for a test:

- Write the test for the code that uses the expected outcome
- Start modifying existing code that is being tested
- Run the test and make sure it passes

Repeat the three steps above until you are happy the refactor is complete.

Commitment to Peer Review

Every place I have worked at that had a strong testing culture was also heavily committed to peer reviews of code. To me, peer review means someone else looks at my code to verify it is accomplishing the desired outcome before it goes into production. If you do nothing else other than adding peer review of code to your development practices, the quality and–more importantly–the purpose of your code will improve immensely.

When related to the primary goal, we end up with a workflow like this:

- Developer is writing code to solve a problem
- Developer includes tests (hopefully using TDD, but test-after has value)
- Developer indicates code is ready
- Peer reviews the code, checking for tests and correct intent of code
- With peer approval, code moves to the next target environment

Now, there is something I feel is really important to stress here–it's supposed to be peer review, not superior review. If we're going to be honest, most people do not like being told the code they worked on isn't any good. I used to be extremely defensive about the code I wrote and the ideas associated with those decisions. It made peer review way more stressful than it needed to be because I wasted more time arguing and trying to justify my choices rather than understanding the criticism being presented.

To be clear, code reviews are often very political and can reflect the power dynamics that exist in the project or workplace. You have to work very hard to make them not end up that way! Remember, you are supposed to be reviewing the ideas and implementation, not using it as an opportunity to pump up your own ego or tear down a coworker with whom you might have personal issues with.

Consistency in Development Environments

In my 20+ years of software development, I've used all sorts of different development environments:

- Shared server used by the entire development team
- Virtual servers maintained by the systems department
- PCs on our desk configured to simulate production using FreeBSD jails[1]
- Virtual machines using Vagrant[2]
- Whatever I wanted to install on my own laptop

Obviously, not all of these environments are optimal. Sometimes you have no choice–the decision is made by someone over whom you have no control. But it is obvious not having everyone use the same development environment is a sure way to end up with weird bugs.

Test-centric cultures focus on repeatable processes, and having an easy-to-recreate development environment for people to work in is something definitely worth the time investment. Why? You're trying to eliminate, "It works on my machine," from the list of reasons why stuff isn't working.

The key here is to make sure everyone is using the same building blocks.

Automation Is Your Friend

One of the other concepts I spend a lot of time promoting is the idea of using automation to help you accomplish tasks more quickly. If I find myself doing something manually more than a handful of times, it's a sign this is a task that can definitely benefit from automation.

In an era where we have tools like Vagrant and Docker at our disposal, allowing us to create environments for our code to run in, why do you want to rely on humans to do repetitive tasks? Computers are great at doing what we tell them, over and over again. It just makes sense to script as much as you can.

---

[1] *FreeBSD jails: https://en.wikipedia.org/wiki/FreeBSD_jail*
[2] *Vagrant: https://vagrantup.com*

A process for automatically generating a development environment also means when a developer accidentally messes up their environment (I have lost track of the number of times this has happened), you can quickly get back to a known good state. This frees up developers to experiment, knowing there won't be hours of downtime if they make a mistake.

Pretty much every programming language has automation tools, so chances are you won't have to learn another language to help build out your automation efforts.

Same Languages and Tools

The most important one of these issues is likely making sure everyone is using the same version of the chosen programming language. If your chosen language also supports extensions or add-on libraries, make sure everyone is using the same ones there, too! It seems like such an easy thing to do, but with every developer having their own personal policies about this sort of thing, it's almost inevitable some drift will occur if there are not strict procedures in place.

This should be applied to the other complementary pieces of your application: database servers, caching servers, build tools for minifying and compressing things. Being consistent this way also eliminates weird bugs due to different versions of tools behaving in slightly different ways.

I am a believer in always using the latest, stable version of every tool the application uses. That way, you get to take advantage of any updates for bug fixes or patching of security issues. The longer you hold off on updating the tools your application uses, the more likely you are to either get compromised or be in a position where an upgrade to the latest stable version of things is a nightmare. Don't let it get to that point.

Same Practices

This is one I feel is extremely underrated and can often lead to a lot of friction. You're probably familiar with coding standards–how the code itself should be structured in terms of indenting, positioning of braces, brackets, things like that. Most languages have produced community-driven tools that make it easy to enforce or even automatically apply them.

Beyond code style issues, you should also focus on making sure folks are using the same coding practices. This might not be an issue if your language of choice follows the "there is only one way to do it" path, but languages that mix procedural and object-oriented and functional practices (like PHP) give bored programmers lots of options to create code that is hard to maintain going forward.

Pick some coding practices you're happy with and make sure to enforce them via code reviews. The consistency in structures and practices will make it easier to spot when something has gone wrong, instead of having to make mental context switches to adjust to someone else's style.

Like so many things involved with test-centric culture, you are doing a bunch of work upfront to gain big benefits down the road.

Trust

Finally, I need to talk to you about trust. When you look at the practices I am advocating, it sure seems like I am not trusting you to do the "right thing" as expressed by all these rules:

- We review code, so you understand what everyone else is doing.

- We write tests for everything because you need confidence things work.

- We write code in the same style, so you have less friction in naming things.

- We write code using the same practices, so you can debug things easier.

- We automate things, so you don't zone out and make a critical mistake.

In other words, I am trying to put you in a position to succeed! Test-centric cultures can be built; it just takes a lot of work and will require you (and others) to change what you've been doing.

It took a terrible development experience and crazy amounts of overtime (like 120 hours in six weeks) in 2003 for me to come around and start making the changes I felt I needed to make sure it would never happen again. I pushed hard to instill a lot of the practices I outlined above. Some of it worked, some of it didn't, and I left when I realized I wasn't going to get my way.

Ever since, I have worked very hard to implement these same practices everywhere I went, wanting to trust that my coworkers thought these things were just as important as I did. It didn't always work, but whenever I left, I felt I had put in an effort to change things. That's all I ever really wanted.

Chapter

14

Bootstrapping

Most modern PHP web application frameworks use the front controller design pattern[1] to handle incoming requests. The use of this design pattern is also frequently accompanied by the use of code which "bootstraps" your application.

---

[1] front controller design pattern: _https://en.wikipedia.org/wiki/Front_controller_

14. Bootstrapping

This is the section of your application where you're probably doing things like initializing databases, setting environment variables, or adding things to the service locator. In short, this work is critical to making your application run.

Naturally, a lot of your code relies on things being done in bootstrapping, so for testing purposes, we need to create a bootstrapping sequence of our own. Previous releases of OpenCFP[2] used to have to do a lot more work as part of the bootstrapping sequence, but a massive refactor towards making it more "Symfony-like" eliminated some of those issues.

By default, PHPUnit will look for a phpunit.xml file in the same directory where it's being run. You can write lots and lots of tests and never need to do anything at all with one of these configuration files. When you do need something specific to your application to help your tests, this is the file to create and modify as required.

For OpenCFP here is what that file looks like:

```
1.  <phpunit
2.      xmlns:xsi="http://www.w3.org/2001/XMLSchema-instance"
3.      xsi:noNamespaceSchemaLocation="vendor/phpunit/phpunit/phpunit.xsd"
4.      backupGlobals="false"
5.      backupStaticAttributes="false"
6.      bootstrap="vendor/autoload.php"
7.      colors="true"
8.      columns="max"
9.      verbose="true"
10.     convertErrorsToExceptions="true"
11.     convertNoticesToExceptions="true"
12.     convertWarningsToExceptions="true"
13.     processIsolation="false"
14.     stopOnFailure="false"
15. >
16.     <php>
17.         <env name="COLUMNS" value="120"/>
18.         <ini name="memory_limit" value="-1"/>
19.         <server name="CFP_ENV" value="testing"/>
20.         <env name="CFP_ENV" value="testing"/>
21.         <env name="KERNEL_CLASS" value="OpenCFP\Kernel"/>
22.     </php>
23.     <filter>
24.         <whitelist>
25.             <directory>src</directory>
26.         </whitelist>
```

[2] OpenCFP: https://github.com/opencfp/opencfp

```
27.    </filter>
28.    <testsuites>
29.      <testsuite name="unit">
30.        <directory>tests/Unit</directory>
31.      </testsuite>
32.      <testsuite name="integration">
33.        <directory>tests/Integration</directory>
34.      </testsuite>
35.    </testsuites>
36.    <listeners>
37.        <listener class="Symfony\Bridge\PhpUnit\SymfonyTestsListener"/>
38.    </listeners>
39. </phpunit>
```

For the purposes of bootstrapping, there are two parts of the file I want to talk about.

Test Environment Bootstrapping

In the phpunit.xml file, any file put into the bootstrap attribute will get executed whenever you start running tests. For OpenCFP, this means loading our Composer autoloading script. In an older version of OpenCFP, this is the file that the bootstrap value was set to:

```php
1.  /**
2.   * @param array          $basePath
3.   * @param Environment $environment
4.   */
5.  public function __construct($basePath, Environment $environment)
6.  {
7.      parent::__construct();
8.
9.      $this['path'] = $basePath;
10.     $this['env'] = $environment;
11.
12.     $this->bindPathsInApplicationContainer();
13.     $this->bindConfiguration();
14.
15.     // Register Gateways...
16.     $this->register(new WebGatewayProvider);
17.     $this->register(new ApiGatewayProvider);
18.     $this->register(new OAuthGatewayProvider);
19.
20.     // Services...
21.     $this->register(new SessionServiceProvider);
22.     $this->register(new FormServiceProvider);
23.     $this->register(new UrlGeneratorServiceProvider);
```

```
24.    $this->register(new ControllerResolverServiceProvider);
25.    $this->register(new DatabaseServiceProvider);
26.    $this->register(new ValidatorServiceProvider);
27.    $this->register(new TranslationServiceProvider);
28.    $this->register(new MonologServiceProvider, [
29.        'monolog.logfile' => $this->config('log.path') ?: "{$basePath}/log/app.log",
30.        'monolog.name' => 'opencfp',
31.        'monlog.level' => strtoupper(
32.            $this->config('log.level') ?: 'debug'
33.        ),
34.    ]);
35.    $this->register(new SwiftmailerServiceProvider, [
36.        'swiftmailer.options' => [
37.            'host' => $this->config('mail.host'),
38.            'port' => $this->config('mail.port'),
39.            'username' => $this->config('mail.username'),
40.            'password' => $this->config('mail.password'),
41.            'encryption' => $this->config('mail.encryption'),
42.            'auth_mode' => $this->config('mail.auth_mode'),
43.        ],
44.    ]);
45.
46.    $this->register(new SentryServiceProvider);
47.    $this->register(new TwigServiceProvider);
48.    $this->register(new HtmlPurifierServiceProvider);
49.    $this->register(new SpotServiceProvider);
50.    $this->register(new ImageProcessorProvider);
51.    $this->register(new ResetEmailerServiceProvider());
52.
53.    // Application Services...
54.    $this->register(new ApplicationServiceProvider);
55.
56.    $this->registerGlobalErrorHandler($this);
57. }
```

Being a Silex[3] application at the time, the bootstrapping focuses on using a global Application object, then initializing a bunch of services, telling this globally-available object about it. For testing purposes, we will sometimes need to substitute our own values. Let's take a look at how one of the older tests (one for the application's DashboardController object) sets things up.

First, we create our Application object and tell it we're in testing mode. Next, we set the session object in the application to be a fake object.

---

[3] Silex: http://silex.sensiolabs.org

```
$app = new Application(BASE_PATH, Environment::testing());
$app['session'] = new Session(new MockFileSessionStorage());
```

There is a tendency for testers who like to employ test doubles to sometimes forget you can use a fake object instead of creating a stub or mock. In this case, we're using a fake from the Symfony project.

Our application used Sentry[4] for handling authentication and authorization, so I needed to create a test double for this particular test.

```
1.  // Set things up so Sentry believes we're logged in
2.  $user = m::mock('StdClass');
3.  $user->shouldReceive('id')->andReturn(1);
4.  $user->shouldReceive('getId')->andReturn(1);
5.  $user->shouldReceive('hasAccess')->with('admin')->andReturn(true);
6.
7.  // Create a test double for Sentry
8.  $sentry = m::mock('StdClass');
9.  $sentry->shouldReceive('check')->times(3)->andReturn(true);
10. $sentry->shouldReceive('getUser')->andReturn($user);
11. $app['sentry'] = $sentry;
```

The dashboard controller is expecting there to be a profile for the user and a talk associated with the user.

```
1.  // Create a test double for a talk in profile
2.  $talk = m::mock('StdClass');
3.  $talk->shouldReceive('title')->andReturn('Test Title');
4.  $talk->shouldReceive('id')->andReturn(1);
5.  $talk->shouldReceive('type', 'category', 'created_at');
6.
7.  // Create a test double for profile
8.  $profile = m::mock('StdClass');
9.  $profile->shouldReceive('name')->andReturn('Test User');
10. $profile->shouldReceive(
11.   'photo', 'company', 'twitter', 'airport', 'bio', 'info', 'transportation', 'hotel'
12. );
13. $profile->shouldReceive('talks')->andReturn([$talk]);
14.
15. $speakerService = m::mock('StdClass');
16. $speakerService->shouldReceive('findProfile')->andReturn($profile);
17.
18. $app['application.speakers'] = $speakerService;
```

[4] Sentry: https://cartalyst.com/manual/sentry/2.1

I hope you're noticing the pattern here:

- Create a stand-in for an existing dependency
- Tell the `Application` object to use it

Now that we're done bootstrapping, we actually "run" the application, use output buffering to prevent output which can mess up the test output, and then run through our testing scenario.

```
 1. ob_start();
 2. $app->run();  // Fire before handlers... boot...
 3. ob_end_clean();
 4.
 5. // Instantiate the controller and run the indexAction
 6. $controller = new \OpenCFP\Http\Controller\DashboardController();
 7. $controller->setApplication($app);
 8.
 9. $response = $controller->showSpeakerProfile();
10. $this->assertContains('Test Title', (string) $response);
11. $this->assertContains('Test User', (string) $response);
```

I know I went through a lot of code, but go back and think about the basics of creating bootstrapping sequences for your tests:

- Pay attention to dependencies set in the application itself
- Create substitutes for those dependencies
- Set them in your test setup

Like so many other things, when you start writing tests for your code, design decisions which make building the application easier through global "application" objects often mean extra work when it comes time to test things.

Auto-Wiring Bootstrapping

The examples in the previous section are for an older app using a pattern that is perhaps not so common with PHP web application frameworks that are popular as I write this in the winter of 2019-2020. OpenCFP has evolved as well to take advantage of the "most batteries included" approach Symfony takes. Instead of all that work (which is many lines of code that I have to support) of a custom bootstrapping sequence, I can use the application's "kernel" to do all the work of creating dependencies for me.

In the phpunit.xml file, there is a section where you can set environment variables PHP can see. In the current version of OpenCFP, it looks like this:

```
<php>
    <env name="COLUMNS" value="120"/>
    <ini name="memory_limit" value="-1"/>
    <server name="CFP_ENV" value="testing"/>
    <env name="CFP_ENV" value="testing"/>
    <env name="KERNEL_CLASS" value="OpenCFP\Kernel"/>
</php>
```

So, to take advantage of what I can only describe as "auto-wiring bootstrapping," we set an environment variable that points to our custom Symfony kernel via KERNEL_CLASS. This is used by a base test case object provided by the symfony/framework-bundle package. If I create other test objects by extending from this base test case object, some magic behind the scenes runs all the code in my custom kernel, meaning I should have access to almost everything my code-under-test is expecting to be available.

This means my tests avoid having to explicitly do all the work that the older test bootstrapping did. This does means that maybe some dependencies get created that my particular test will not need, but I view not having to maintain multiple bootstrap-and-initialize sections (often with only minor differences between them) as a bonus.

One of the reasons to go with a web application framework is to take advantage of tools that have been created to solve common problems a programmer faces. If a framework gives you tools to make writing tests easier, use them! The kernel for Symfony allows you to reduce the amount of bootstrapping work you do and the ability to modify facades at run-time for testing Laravel-based applications spring to mind.

Chapter

15

No Tests? No Problem!

The default state for most PHP applications is not to have any automated tests. In the past, I would have started talking about a lack of professionalism or even frame it as a moral failure when discussing this. This is, of course, a terrible way to be. Instead, it's better to focus on how you can get from no tests to at least one test and hopefully pointed in the direction of having more tests.

How Did We End Up Without Any Tests?

There are two major forces that lead applications toward not having any tests. The first is that it's hard to teach beginners in a language how to use testing tools; they are still learning the language itself! Since tests are code that has to be written in a specific way with specific tools, it shouldn't come as a surprise that people do struggle on their own to figure it all out. Tests are just code that shows how to use other code; it's a very abstract concept for beginners to understand. Don't worry; you can get there.

The second force is the work-culture pressure that says you don't have time to write tests. I once quit a job because I kept getting told this. Of course, the codebase was full of bugs and difficult to debug. One of the reasons this attitude toward testing is so damaging is because you end up spending more time fixing the bugs that make it into your application in production than if you had been "given permission" for tests to be written. There are plenty of actual studies out there now that demonstrate the value of writing tests for your application as you go. Use your favorite search engine and look for "TDD study." You'll be surprised by what you find.

Putting all that aside for the time being, you've now decided you want to start writing tests for your application. Great! I want to share some strategies that have worked well for myself and others.

Bug Fixes Need Proof

One strategy that has worked well for myself and others is to implement a policy requiring all bug fixes to have one or more tests that can be automated to prove the bug was actually fixed. The process for this is usually something similar to the following:

First, a bug is reported, and someone verifies the problem being reported is actually a bug. Sometimes it's simply an unexpected outcome or a complaint about the user experience. We all know, "It's broken!" is not always a bug report, but often a statement of frustration.

Armed with proof that there is a bug ready to fix, the next step should be to write a test that assumes the bug does not exist. Using the conditions under which the bug occurs, you create a test which assumes (like all tests) everything is working correctly. The test should fail because of the bug! You then continue with the normal TDD cycle of re-running the test as you make changes to the code until the test passes.

Now you have a test that is proof this bug no longer exists! Also, hopefully, you have not broken something in another part of your application. If that happens, you write another test to verify this new problem (the technical term is a regression) is fixed and then verify the test you wrote for the initial bug fix still passes. Test suites are your number one weapon against regressions in your code; you don't want to always break old code when you make changes!

New Features Require Proof

Another strategy for tests is to require all new features to have a test proving the new feature works as expected. This differs from the "bug fixes" strategy in that you will often end up writing multiple tests to prove a new feature works correctly. This strategy is where you get to see the power of TDD as a tool for design code that should be easy to test.

So how do you do this? You need to begin by deciding how you will prove, at the code level, the feature is working. Do you need a new object with a new method that returns a specific value? Are you using existing code? Yes, you might have to do a little work up front to figure out how you're going to make this new feature work. But that is where TDD shines!

The next step is to write a test assuming the new or modified code works correctly. Of course, the test will fail! Again, just like when you are working with tests to verify bug fixes, you keep writing code and running the tests until they all pass. Now you have one or more tests that verify this new feature is working as expected at the code level.

Also, just like with the bug fix strategy, there is likely a chance these changes have caused a regression elsewhere in your codebase. Make sure to do some thorough checking of things using the application itself in areas that have been deemed critical.

Test Suites Are Not Bulletproof

At this point, you're beginning to have a test suite that covers some portion of your application and helps provide limited protection against regressions. Be careful not to be lulled into a false sense of security by any number of passing tests. After all, these tests are written by humans instead of super-intelligent AIs seeking to move us toward a life of leisure in a land of plenty.

Tests only cover the scenarios the writer could think of at the time they were written. Yes, it is entirely possible to have a test suite with 100% coverage of your code (meaning every line of code in your application was executed as part of a test) and still have an application that does not work correctly.

You need a wide variety of tests–unit tests for individual objects, integration tests to verify these objects interact correctly with each other, and some functional tests (perhaps done manually) to make sure the application works correctly.

A test suite with high levels of coverage allows you to focus on solving problems with some level of confidence that you will not introduce new bugs into an existing system.

Now get out there and start building those test suites!

Chapter

16

Nobody Is Running the Tests!

This is one of the more interesting situations I have come across–an application with a large test suite nobody uses! I have come across this a few times, and the explanations are usually the same.

Time Pressure

"We were in a rush to get a bunch of features done, and continuing to write tests was slowing us down, so we stopped." Ah yes, time, the slayer of developer's dreams. The only thing we can never make any more of.

Given my experiences with development pushes, it is incredibly likely you spent more time fixing the bugs introduced by the abnormal work conditions than if you had continued with the slow-and-steady pace TDD advocates.

What can be done to help with this? A firm commitment to the continued use of tests as a way to validate your code is working as expected, even in the face of intimidation or threats from stakeholders.

I realize this will not be easy. I have been accused of being reckless by some folks when insisting tests be a non-negotiable part of your developer workflow. "I'll get fired for suggesting it!"

That is not my intention! My intention is to present the argument that some kind of crazy overtime schedule to meet a deadline will end up with more mistakes in the code than if a more measured pace had been used.

Tests Are Too Slow

Test suites should run quickly; quicker runs mean quicker feedback and more time to actually write code. I've worked on projects where running the test suite took over an hour. Nobody wins in that scenario. People become reluctant to run test suites as part of their normal workflow.

Imagine a process like this:

- Developer writes tests while working on a new feature
- Developer runs the tests for that feature until everything passes
- Developer then runs the entire test suite to make sure nothing else breaks

How many times would you get to the third step and say, "Screw it, I'm not sitting here for an hour." This is how slow tests ruin all the work you put into other parts of the test suite.

What kind of conditions lead to a really slow test suite?

I struggled with finding a way to describe the idea I am trying to express accurately. A sizeable portion of my fellow testing evangelists dislike the idea of using test doubles. They complain about all the extra code they need to write in their tests, how easy the doubles can get out of sync with the dependencies they are representing, the overall "brittleness" of tests that rely on doubles, and a number of other complaints not worth rehashing here.

Their solution is to create fakes (which are doubles but in disguise) or to use the real thing whenever possible. I don't really object to this technique–using real dependencies is a good thing!

The side effect of refusing to use test doubles is you start picking up what I have labeled "outside actor" costs. These are the tiny bits of extra time (and sometimes extra memory) your tests pick up whenever they talk to real databases or real web services. When your test suite is small, it's more like a speed bump than anything. Once your test suite starts covering large parts of a large application, you will notice it.

At this point, you might become conflicted. On the one hand, you want to make sure your application has sufficient test coverage to catch regressions and allow you to write new code easier. On the other hand, you want your test suite to be lightning-fast, so developers aren't sitting around waiting for their tests to finish running.

Monolithic Bootstrapping

Most web application frameworks are built around the front controller[1] design pattern. Part of using this pattern is also a bootstrapping sequence that takes place before the incoming request is handled. Often, there is a lot going on in there, and that means a lot of work for you to in the "arrange" step of the Arrange-Act-Assert[2] testing pattern. Of course, there are testing patterns; developers aren't the only ones to get in on the pattern fun.

What can we do? Well, one way I have found is to break down your bootstrapping sequence from one monolithic method doing a bunch of work into a smaller method that calls a series of other small methods that do all the bootstrapping. You are in a much better position to figure out what parts of the bootstrapping sequence are absolutely necessary for the code you're trying to test.

Shared Testing Environments

This is not the problem it used to be, thanks to the rapid adoption of technologies like virtual machines and containers. These tools can be used to replicate the environment your code is likely to run in on your own computer. I upgraded from a mid-2012 Mac Book Air to a late-2016 Mac Book Pro in early 2017 (yes, with the cool little touch bar) because I

---

[1]   front controller: _https://en.wikipedia.org/wiki/Front_controller_
[2]   Arrange-Act-Assert: _http://wiki.c2.com/?ArrangeActAssert_

found myself running out of resources all the time due to the demands of the modern development environments I find myself needing to use.

So what happens when there is a shared development environment in place:

- All the developers on the project do their work and maybe run individual tests
- At some point, they need to merge their work and run the entire test suite
- The shared environment combusts because of load
- The testing suite randomly crashes due to race conditions on shared resources like databases

Yes, I have been there. You end up with a terrible loop of behavior where people don't run the tests until the last minute possible because the shared environment crashes when everyone is trying to run their tests at the last minute. This continues pretty much forever until enough people quit that the load on the shared environment doesn't matter, or someone spends a bunch of time learning Vagrant[3] or Docker[4] and forces everyone to switch.

---

[3] Vagrant: *https://vagrantup.com*
[4] Docker: *https://docker.com*

Chapter

17

"You're Not Getting Paid to Test!"

Many times I have heard from people who work at agencies or as free-lancers that they get a lot of pushback when the topic of testing comes up. You tell me, "I am having trouble convincing the client the value of tests," and I totally understand. I'm often told, "Chris, clients see an item on the invoice about tests, and they start complaining!"

What can you do about this? I want to share with you some strategies I think can help.

Testing Is Part of the Job

We're past the point where you can reasonably claim the person who writes code has no responsibility to test it. Even if you are not using automated tests, you are still testing what you've done! Are you adding "testing in the browser" as a line item in the invoice you submit? You will have to forgive my ignorance surrounding current client invoicing practices, but it strikes me as very unlikely.

I'm not so militant that I am going to tell you, you're not a professional if you don't write tests because that ship sailed a very, very long time ago. The bottom line is you need to have some type of repeatable test for the work you're doing for others.

If you are in the position to use a web application framework not invented in-house, then you are likely using things that have automated tests you can run. But, you aren't "allowed" to write tests for the other stuff you're doing?

So my advice is to write the tests and include them as part of the work you are doing. If questioned about it, there isn't any other answer to give than, "Tests are part of what I am delivering, so it will not break after I am no longer involved." I realize you will encounter some very aggressive clients who will proclaim you are expected to deliver bug-free products to them. I cannot think of any way to reduce the number of bugs that appear, other than to make sure you have tests to verify everything works as expected.

Lost Opportunity Costs

This is a topic that has become a personal favorite of mine because it is so relatable to non-technical types. It focuses on pointing out that bugs making it into production will actually cost you money. Here's how it works.

A developer is working on a new feature. If they were to find a bug, now is the cheapest time to fix it–and having automated tests to verify things aren't broken is a good way to do this. But they don't have tests, so they're the best they can. Despite their best efforts, they create a bug.

The next step is getting a coworker to check their code via a review. If the reviewer finds a bug, then our valiant developer has to go back and fix it. This costs time and money. Once they think they've fixed the problem, then it has to go back to the reviewer. In this case, the reviewer gives them the thumbs up, and the code can proceed to QA.

But what if there were some tests? I'm willing to bet the introduced bug would have a very high chance of getting caught before the code gets to the reviewer. Chances are the review goes more smoothly and costs less in time and resources.

Now, if a bug is found during manual testing by QA, well, the cost to fix it is now significantly higher. Consider that this is now the flow:

- Developer implements feature, no bugs found
- Code is reviewed, no bugs found
- QA finds bug
- Developer goes back, hopefully, fixes the bug
- Code is reviewed, no bugs found
- QA does not find a bug

That's three extra steps, and those steps are not free in terms (again, I can't stress this enough) of time and/or money.

Let's say the code makes it all the way into production, and there's a bug found by the customer. The cost of fixing this could be cheap:

- Developer implements feature, no bugs found
- Code is reviewed, no bugs found
- QA does not find bug
- Customer finds the bug
- Developer goes back, hopefully, fixes the bug
- Code is reviewed, no bugs found
- QA does not find a bug
- Customer does not find a bug

That was eight steps in total, but sometimes there are bugs that are really expensive. They could cost you ten times what the developer's time costs. It might even ruin your company. I'm fortunate that only once in my career did I release code into production with a bug so bad the whole application got taken down. It was not a pleasant experience.

So, the lack of tests is not only causing you to spend more money to fix bugs as they show up in more expensive parts of the process, having to go back and fix those bugs is actually causing you to miss out on other work.

What about new features? Can't — fixing bugs. What about going back and refactoring some code to use a new library? Can't — fixing bugs. What about some custom work for a client? Can't — fixing bugs.

I'm sure you're starting to spot a theme here.

The value of having your developers write tests that can be automated is that you are far more likely to find bugs before they get into production. That is the ultimate goal of testing–moving code swiftly out of the developer's environment and into production where it is fulfilling the goals of the application.

Chapter

18

It's About People

I asked developers who actually do testing to send me some thoughts or questions I could address.

Like Kids on a Playground

> *"Dev teams tend to be babies about testing; they need a push from the top to start doing it. For example, if a parent is not okay with their kid eating dirt but doesn't say anything, and the other kids on the playground don't say anything, it doesn't matter if one little kid tells the kid not to and tells the other kids not to. They just become 'bossy' and 'annoying' and need to 'chill'."*

This is a great example of how changes need to come from the top and be reinforced by people closer to the development team. Let's face it; most people will do the minimum required to get the job done. Before people get mad at me, please don't email me examples of your high-functioning team where everyone embraces testing. Your team is an outlier; be happy.

So what can be done to improve this scenario? It's going to require a lot of effort to both implement the testing of code as a policy and to keep them doing it. Asking people to write some kind of repeatable tests for their code is reasonable. Many people consider this sort of thing to be a bare minimum requirement for being a programmer.

Be firm and make test-centric policies a non-negotiable part of your development workflow. Many developers are battling a natural instinct to resist change when presented with Test-Driven Development. Guide them and help them understand TDD and testing practices will soon feel as natural as other programming techniques they didn't previously understand but now embrace.

Lack of Good Docs

> *"Other reasons are much more interesting. One is the perceived lack of good docs. For instance, most documentation about unit testing uses a simple example, which is fine for understanding the concept, but it lacks a real-world application. Some developers actually want to use TDD, but they fear the project would be too hard to test because there isn't very much good documentation about testing a complex system."*

I have struggled with trying to find a good approach to this one over the years. It's true–most examples of how to write unit tests are extremely simple. Providing people with more complicated answers can be hard because everyone's codebases are a little different and present unique challenges.

For example, my mentioned-too-many-times project OpenCFP has the constraint of needing to always account for a global application object with parts which need to be over-ridden and redefined just to test parts of the application. It's non-intuitive to know that unless you understand your tests are meant to be doing a lot of things similar to what your application should be doing.

This is getting to the heart of the biggest problem of teaching people about testing. It's almost impossible to give people generic advice about what they should do! Sure, there are some guiding principles we can look at like Arrange-Act-Assert[1] or encouraging people not to abuse test doubles, but it's not enough.

It's ironic that despite the ridiculous amount of information available at our fingertips via the internet, the best way to teach people about unit testing is actually to sit down next to someone and guide them through the task.

Convincing People About Time

> *"My team is considering integrating unit tests into our development process. Until now, we have only experimented in a rather small prototype setting. In theory, I totally agree with you, but in practice, I haven't seen the benefits yet. Writing these tests defi-nitely costs us time. I wonder if this really pays off. At least it feels slow because you end up spending half your time writing tests. Do you really get this time back?"*

It's an entirely fair question: Am I going to see a benefit from the time I am spending writing tests? I'm pretty sure you know what my opinion on this is, but let's dig a bit deeper into the issue.

This person correctly identified that writing tests takes time. After all, you are spending time thinking about how to test something. Then you have to spend time writing the test and iterating over the test while you write them and making sure you have covered all your branches and conditions and where did all the time go?!

That time went to you being a little more deliberate and thoughtful about the problem you were trying to solve! Those tests you spent time writing are there to make sure you didn't accidentally break something else. They are also there for the next time code gets changed elsewhere, and it breaks. Except you'll find out during the actual coding work, instead of at the end of a long day when your attention is not what it should be, and maybe you're tired and want to go home.

---

[1]   Arrange-Act-Assert: http://wiki.c2.com/?ArrangeActAssert

I feel the need to circle back to the idea of "lost opportunity costs." The idea is that the use of TDD will lead to code with fewer bugs making it into production. That means you can then continue to work on other tasks, like new features or a much-needed refactoring of a key subsystem.

Not to mention the beneficial side effect of making it easier to modify existing code with confidence. Why? The tests will let you know if you've broken something! This allows us to continue with a cycle of forward progress, instead of feeling like you are in a permanent state of emergency with respect to bug fixing.

Cowboys Above Me

"How do you sell testing when your bosses are cowboy coders?"

There was a time when my reaction to someone complaining about their job or terrible processes was to snap off a quick, "Well, you should quit your job!" I've softened my stance on this over the years, but I think this scenario is definitely one where it's warranted.

Basically, you don't want to work for people like this. Unless you really don't care about the work you're doing. In that case, you should also quit your job.

This is not about professionalism or software craftsmanship. It's about understanding that an environment where you are not encouraged to be thoughtful about the work you're doing—and discouraged from the use of tools and practices that lead to repeatable success—is toxic.

I have worked in enough toxic environments over the years, and they all had many things in common. Learn to recognize when the place you work is going to hold you back instead of allowing you to grow both as a programmer and as a person.

Like I said, testing is really about people.

Index

A

API, 31, 41, 74, 77–80, 82, 90, 93
  building, 78
  call, 12
  publicly-available, 74
  Schema Validation, 77, 79, 81
  testing, 73–74, 76, 78, 80, 82
  third-party, 89
application
  legacy, 109
  real-world, 136
automation, 7, 12, 99, 111
  browser, 96

B

Behat, 96
Behavioural-Driven Development, 96
Beizer, Boris, 5
Bergmann, Sebastian, 16, 18–20, 22–23,
71–72, 76–77, 81–82, 91–92, 94
bootstrapping, 115–18, 120, 129
  sequence, 116, 120, 129
  test environment, 117, 119
bugs
  production, 97–98
  tests for, 108–9
  type-related, 101–2

C

CircleCI, 99
code
  coverage, 100–101
  cutting-and-pasting, 12
  duplicated, 87
  linter, 99
  mutated, 104
  refactor, 53
  release, 133
  reviews, 98
  style issues, 112
  testable, 73
  type-hinted, 40
Codeception, 96
Composer, 17, 71, 79, 99–100
  installed, 17
constructor, 27–28, 32, 37
  parameter, 28, 90
controller, 115, 120, 129
  front, 129
coverage, 6, 101, 109, 125

D

database
  initializing, 116
  in-memory, 63
  migrations, 11, 99

data providers
  annotation, 47
  method, 46, 86
  simple, 86
debugger, 100
dependencies, development, 79, 104
deployments, 74, 98–99
development environments, 111–12
  modern, 130
  shared, 130
Docker, 111, 130
doubles, 7
  multiple, 40

E

environment variables, 116, 121

F

file
  basic test case, 20
  mutated, 104
  phpunit.xml, 116
fizzbuzz, 84–87
functional tests, 7, 125

G

Git, 11
GitHub Actions, 99

I

IBM, 10, 97
Infection, 104

J

Jenkins, 99
JsonPlaceHolder, 90, 93

M

Microsoft, 10, 97
mock, 26
  objects, 28, 71
Mockery, 26
Mutation Code Coverage, 105
mutations, 104–5

O

object-relation mappers (ORMs), 11, 99
OpenAPI, 77–78
  definition, 77
  schema, 78
  Specification (OAS), 77–78, 82

P

PHAR (PHP Archive), 16
PHPStan, 101–3
PHPUnit
  install, 16–17
  Test Cases, 21, 23
  Test Runner, 17, 19
  website, 16, 42
Prophecy, 26, 28, 31, 33, 36–37, 70–71
  framework, 26
Psalm, 101–3
pyswagger, 78
Python, 74, 78

Q

Quality Assurance (QA), 98, 132–33

R

refactoring, 28, 49, 51, 53, 98, 100, 110, 134

S

Scryfall, 74

servers, 12, 77, 99

  caching, 112

  continuous integration, 12

  web, 97

services

  remote, 77

  web, 129

Silex, 118

Speccy, 78–79

spies, 28, 33, 40

Sturgeon, Phil, 78

Sussman, Noah, 6

Swagger, 78

Symfony, 80, 117, 121

T

TDD (Test-Driven Development), 3, 10, 41–42, 44, 46, 48, 50, 52, 54, 56–57, 59, 97, 100, 109–10, 136

  study, 124

teamcity, 71–72, 76–77, 81–82, 91–92, 94

test

  automated, 12, 98, 123, 132

  double, 11–12, 25–26, 28, 30, 32, 34, 36, 38, 40, 44, 63, 70, 119, 128–29

  integration, 7, 125

  spies, 28–29, 31, 33–35

  suites, 6, 10, 16, 124–25, 128

  unit, 2, 7, 71, 79, 89, 91, 109, 125, 136–37

test cases

  advanced, 44

  basic, 21

  passing, 19

tools

  automation, 99, 112

  code generation, 77

  static analysis, 101–2

  testing, 77, 96, 104, 124

Trask, Matthew, 78

Travis CI, 99

Twig, 102

V

Vagrant, 111, 130

  time learning, 130

W

work-culture pressure, 124

X

XDebug, 100

Feedback and Updates

Please let us know what you thought of this book! What did you enjoy? What was confusing or could have been improved? Did you find errata? Any feedback and thoughts you have regarding this book will help us improve a future edition.

To leave a review, go to https://phpa.me/grumpy-testing-book

Follow the Author

Chris Hartjes is active on twitter, @grmpyprogrammer, and shares his experiences, lessons, and advice on testing and programming.

Updates

To keep in touch and be notified about future editions to this book, visit http://phparch.com and sign up for our (low-volume) mailing list.

You can also follow us on twitter @phparch as well as on facebook: https://facebook.com/phparch/

php[architect] Books

The php[architect] series of books cover topics relevant to modern PHP programming. We offer most of our books in both print and digital formats. Print copy price includes free shipping to the US. Books sold digitally are available to you DRM-free in PDF, ePub, or Mobi formats for viewing on any device that supports these.

To view the complete selection of books and order a copy of your own, please visit: http://phparch.com/books/.

- **The Fizz Buzz Fix: Secrets to Thinking Like an Experienced Developer**
  By Edward Barnard
  ISBN: 978-1940111759

- **The Dev Lead Trenches: Lessons for Managing Developers**
  By Chris Tankersley
  ISBN: 978-1940111711

- **Web Scraping with PHP, 2nd Edition**
  By Matthew Turland
  ISBN: 978-1940111674

- **Security Principles for PHP Applications**
  By Eric Mann
  ISBN: 978-1940111612

- **Docker for Developers, 2nd Edition**
  By Chris Tankersley
  ISBN: 978-1940111568 (Print edition)

- **What's Next? Professional Development Advice**
  Edited by Oscar Merida
  ISBN: 978-1940111513

- **Functional Programing in PHP, 2nd Edition**
  By: Simon Holywell
  ISBN: 978-1940111469

- **Web Security 2016**
  Edited by Oscar Merida
  ISBN: 978-1940111414

- **Building Exceptional Sites with WordPress & Thesis**
  By Peter MacIntyre
  ISBN: 978-1940111315

- **Integrating Web Services with OAuth and PHP**
  By Matthew Frost
  ISBN: 978-1940111261

- **Zend Framework 1 to 2 Migration Guide**
  By Bart McLeod
  ISBN: 978-1940111216

- **XML Parsing with PHP**
  By John M. Stokes
  ISBN: 978-1940111162

- **Zend PHP 5 Certification Study Guide, Third Edition**
  By Davey Shafik with Ben Ramsey
  ISBN: 978-1940111100

- **Mastering the SPL Library**
  By Joshua Thijssen
  ISBN: 978-1940111001

Made in the USA
Monee, IL
05 April 2021